MW01289146

RECOGNIZING
PRINCE HALL

Books by Dan Weatherington

BRANDYWINE BAY

BLEMISHED HARVEST

THE SEVENTH GIFT OF GOD

RECOGNIZING PRINCE HALL

WILLIE

DAN WEATHERINGTON

RECOGNIZING PRINCE HALL

FORWARD BY

RIC CARTER EDITOR

NORTH CAROLINA MASON

Copyright © 2010 by Dan Weatherington

All rights reserved. No part of this book may be reproduced or utilized
in any form or by means, electronic or mechanical, including
photocopying, recording, or by any information storage or retrieval
system, without permission in writing from the publisher.

Printed in the United States of America

Dedicated to the great and noble men of both races who are guided by the principles of Freemasonry and not by the dictates of a backward society.

Foreword

Ric Carter
Editor *North Carolina Mason*

Elementary and high schools teach us that history is a linear thing stuffed into an oversized, heavy-paged book and carrying one truth.

Age teaches us there is no single version of the past. There are as many versions and perspectives as there are participants and witnesses. History holds no objective "truth." Truth is approached only when examining a fabric woven of all those perspectives and remembrances.

Freemasonry is more attached to tradition and habit than most institutions. When the fraternity finally began to break with our national and institutional racial traditions (certainly much later than it should), there was predictable upheaval. The change took place over years. There was no single moment when the tide turned; it did not come as some revelation in the night. It was hard won. The discussions were in the thousands, taking place all over the state and world. The debates were among brothers in their homes, in district and state meetings, on the Internet, in frustrated phone calls, in secret plots, and in public pleadings.

Dan Weatherington was there for much of the discussion and debate. He was talking, listening, arguing with people on all sides of the issue. He was a first person witness and an agitator for change.

Recognizing Prince Hall dips into Dan's reality and gives the reader a look into this sea change in the fraternity. His barely fictionalized story carries an important perspective, one which will add greatly to the intricate weave that will become the history of Freemasonry here.

We should appreciate Weatherington's contribution to writing this history as well as making it.

Ric Carter

Editor
The North Carolina Mason

Prologue

In the early eighteenth century Freemasonry swept through Europe and into the Americas where it became especially popular with the educated and land owning classes. Most the colonials adhered firmly to the codes of secrecy of the organization. But in the South, most of the land owners also owned slaves. And since slaves were considered less than human, no effort was made to conceal the Masonic rituals from those who had driven the Master to his meetings or those who prepared and served the food and beverages.

Ironically, it was the same rules that prohibited writing any of the Masonic ritual that gave rise to Black Masonry. Since everything had to be committed to memory, the same slaves who were being ignored were also memorizing the these supposedly "secret" works.

Equally ironic was the fact that had these activities been written, they would have been more secret since slaves were forbidden to learn how to read and write. The real secret of Masonry for over two hundred years was Black Masonry.

After the Civil War, when it was no longer necessary to keep their Masonic knowledge a secret, these black Masons quickly began forming their own lodges and groups. Just as quickly, the white Masons began denying what was being called Negro Masonry as "real" Masonry. The whites, who had been forming their own "Grand Lodges" open only to whites, now said that any lodge not a part of their Grand Lodge was considered "clandestine". Black Masons too were forming their own grand lodges under the banner of a man named Prince Hall. Not only were members of these "clandestine" lodges not permitted to visit "regular" lodges, but the rules of Masonry had long forbidden any member of a "regular" lodge from visiting a "clandestine" lodge. This "clandestine" rule served the discriminatory needs of white Masons for decades. It would be the end of the twentieth century before this system would begin to end. Only then would individual white state Grand Lodges begin to "recognize" their Prince Hall counterparts effectively removing the "clandestine" label.

This story is set during the late 1990s as the Grand Lodge of North Carolina begins to join the eighty percent of state grand lodges who have recognized Prince Hall Masons as true and legitimate Masons. The process was far from instant and would take over ten years to accomplish.

Chapter 1

Raleigh

I didn't hear the word "Nigger" until I was eleven years old. It's a safe bet that growing up in the segregated South it was said in my presence many times. Some around me may have said it, but it couldn't have been significant because I don't remember it. My parents didn't use the word and I don't remember any of my neighbors ever saying it.

The first time I heard the word, or actually saw it, was on a hot Sunday in downtown Raleigh. I remember it was Sunday because my parents and I had just gotten out of church and we noticed something going on a couple of blocks away at Capitol Square. We were curious so my father drove in that direction.

Just as soon as we began to circle the Capitol my father moaned and said, "oh god, Let's get out of here." But he couldn't. We were in a line of traffic and the off streets were blocked with people. Some of them were wearing white robes and carrying signs saying "Niggers Know Your Place" and "KKK Forever". All we could do was follow the traffic. By the time we approached the other end of Fayetteville Street, the route was lined with men dressed like soldiers, helmets and all, except these uniforms didn't say "US Army" they said "KKK". I didn't understand a thing going on. The people were chanting "Hell No - Hell No". One man even ran up to us screaming "Hell No - Hell No" and pounded on the roof of our car. I was scared. What were these people so angry about?

Like a normal eleven year old unaware of the situation I asked my father what KKK meant. Somewhat whispering, he responded "Ku Klux Klan." With all the commotion I didn't understand why he was whispering. I thought he had said "clown" and said that I didn't think they were funny. Just then my father saw an opening on Dawson Street and jerked the steering wheel to the left and grunted that there wasn't a damn thing funny about them.

I could tell my father was relieved to be out of the "parade" and I was full of questions. The first thing I wanted to know was what is a "Nigger"? It was obvious those KKK people didn't like Niggers, whatever they are.

When we were several blocks away my father pulled the car over to the curb. I can still hear his words. "Davy, Nigger is a word ignorant, uneducated, people call Colored people and I don't want to ever hear you say it."

My father looked at my mother who hadn't said a thing. "In a way it was funny," he said.

"What was funny? Those people scared the daylights out of me." she said.

"I wonder what those Kluckers would have thought if they had have known they had a good Catholic family in their hands. They hate Catholics just about as much as they do Coloreds and Jews." Then I saw him replace the plastic statue of Jesus that was always on the dashboard of our car. Somehow, when he saw those Klu Kluxers it had disappeared under the seat.

It was a day I'll never forget because of the hate I saw in those people's faces. But the one thing I still didn't understand is why did they hate Colored people?

I grew up in a typical 1950s neighborhood in North Carolina which was, and still is, predominately a college and white collar town. Mothers stayed at home and took care of the children and the fathers went to work. I saw Colored people all the time. "Colored people" was what we called Negroes in the 1950s. It would be years before the term "Black" would be acceptable and decades before anyone would hear about an "African American".

There had been Colored people around me all my life. Our maid, Lois, was Colored and meant as much to me as my own mother. My father was in the produce business and had thirty or forty Colored people working at his plant at any time. I knew most of them by name. The hatred I had seen in those Ku Klux people confused me.

I knew there were differences in White people and Colored people. Everywhere I went it was obvious. Colored people sat at the back of the bus. Whenever Lois would take me uptown we would take the bus and the first thing she would do is take me by the hand and guide me to the back of the bus so I could sit with her. I had seen water fountains for "Colored" and "White" all my life. Even in my own father's plant there were separate bathrooms for Colored and White just like there were for men and women. I didn't understand it. I didn't question it. That was just the way it was.

It was about a year after the Ku Klux Klan incident when the whole thing really became real... and personal.

On weekends and during the summer my father would let me work at the plant stacking crates and pouring tomatoes into the grading machine. The $1.25 an hour I made seemed like a fortune to me and the work wasn't that bad.

I was working on the grading machine when I heard the foreman say that the order we were working on needed to be in New York by six o'clock the next morning. New York? Did he say New York? To a Southern boy the two words "New" and "York" in combination were magic. And, this truckload of tomatoes was headed to New York? I knew what needed to be done. I went straight to my father's office. I didn't have any idea that he would let me go, but one thing was certain. If I didn't ask, I certainly wouldn't be going.

I went through the normal teenage "I don't ask for much" things. Actually, I wasn't a teenager. I was only twelve, but at twelve you think you're twenty. My father leaned back in his chair and asked me if I was ready for such a big trip. My answer was a quick "yes". He looked at his work orders and told me that Roosevelt was going to be driving the truck. As soon as I heard that I knew I was halfway there. Roosevelt had been with my father for over twenty years and my father trusted him absolutely. My father told me to go back to work and he would talk to me in a few minutes. I knew that meant he would be phoning my mother. It wasn't long before my name was called over the intercom. I was on my way to New York.

There's very few things as loud as an eighteen-wheeler on the open road, but even the roar of that truck didn't dampen the new adventures of that trip. While Roosevelt was delivering the tomatoes I took my first ride in a New York taxi, an adventure in itself. But I was lucky. The driver wasn't the con-man type I had been warned to avoid. I got the con-man on the way back. The first driver knew I was a kid and from my accent knew I was from the South. He asked me if I had ever been to New York before. When I told him I hadn't, he flipped the meter off and took the kid

from the South to see New York. We saw the Empire State
Building, Avenue of the Americas, Central Park and a dozen
other places I'd only seen on TV and read about in
magazines. It was fantastic!

The only fly in the ointment of an otherwise perfect
adventure was at a roadside restaurant in New Jersey. When
we had stopped, I got out of the truck to get the food. Even
in the North at that time there were some separate entrances
for Colored and White. I, of course, went into the White
entrance. Inside, I was looking at the menu and the man
behind the counter asked if I was riding in that truck with
that Nigger. My father's words of "uneducated" and
"ignorant" rushed through my mind, even as it does today. I
told him that I was in a truck with a Colored man if that's
what he meant and he told me I could go over to the
Colored entrance to order my food. He said that they don't
serve Niggers on the white side of the restaurant even if a
White man is buying it for them.

Not knowing what else to do, I walked out the front
door and went into the side door of the restaurant, the one
marked "Colored". Even today I wish I had told him to
shove his food and his restaurant up where the sun don't

shine, but I sincerely doubt if he would have cared. I still consider it amazing that one of my early lessons in bigotry came from a man in the North.

Chapter 2

It Begins

My life was about as normal as it gets until I was about thirty years old. By both fate and choice I had ended up in the finance business and accepted a job in a small town about fifty miles east of Raleigh. Many of the guys I worked with were Shriners and it appeared to be the best bet going for a social life for my wife and me. Eventually I asked about becoming a Shriner and was told that first I would have to become a Mason. It made no sense to me, but if that was the way it worked, that was the way it was. I quickly discovered, you don't just "join" the Masons. In order to become a Mason, more correctly, a "Master Mason", a man must pass through three "degrees". This is done with the aid of a "coach" who helps one memorize the things necessary to learn to achieve each degree. My coach was a wonderful man named Bruce Helms. He was a long-time and knowledgeable Mason who made the "catechisms" of each degree come to life. Each day I would spend thirty minutes or so with him in his small insurance office memorizing my catechism.

One morning after I had left Helm's office, I stopped by the Mall. When I returned to the parking lot, there was a pamphlet under the windshield wiper of my car, *The Curse of Baphomet*. I saw the pamphlet had something to do with Masonry so I immediately sat down in the car and read it from front to back. At that point there was someplace I had to go, Bruce Helm's office. Though I had already been there that morning, I considered what I had seen in the pamphlet important... very important.

I barged into Helm's office and I'm sure I looked excited. "Bruce, we need to talk," I said as I shoved the pamphlet at him. "What is this?" I asked.

"Oh, I see Mrs. Irma's out and about," Helms said smiling. "I would have thought it was a bit warm for the old dear to be out passing out her poison."

"You know about these things?" I asked. Now I was confused.

"Oh yes, Mrs. Irma's been passing them out for years. They don't mean a thing."

"From what I read, it sounds pretty serious. It says that the Masons worship Satan. I didn't know anything about that."

"David, I've been a Mason over thirty years and I assure you we don't now, nor have we ever worshiped Satan. That's just some silliness the holy rollers made up. It means nothing. Throw the thing away. There's not a word of truth in it."

In a way, I felt relieved, but things were coming at me too quickly. I never had any plans to become a Mason in the first place. I wanted to become a Shriner.

It wasn't only the Bible tract. That very morning I had asked Helms about a Masonic lodge I had seen out on the highway and wondered why no one ever mentioned it. Helm's answer had been simple and matter of fact. "That's a Nigger lodge," he said.

"What do you mean?" I asked.

"You know what a Nigger is don't you?"

"I guess you mean Colored people," I answered not trying to hide my obvious dislike for his word.

"Whichever you want to call them, they aren't real Masons. They just call themselves Masons. Their stuff isn't a thing like ours. They can't even visit our lodge. Like I say... they're not real Masons."

I didn't say anything, but Hester had used the word "Nigger" so easily it concerned me. I had been in this small agricultural town long enough to realize that terms that belittle people were used as easily as words like "apple" and "street". To these people, it was just common English. It did make me uncomfortable, but when in Rome....

"Bruce, I wasn't..."

"No, I can tell from your voice you're still worried about that pamphlet And... the Nig... Black thing. You need to go ahead and satisfy yourself before you go any further. If you don't, it'll be eating at you from now on. I want you to go talk to Ben Rooker. He's the Secretary of the lodge. He's over at the Baptist church. He's the Pastor. I had breakfast with him this morning and he said he'd be in all day. Go ahead and talk to him. I'll call him and tell him you're coming."

I decided to do as Helms had suggested and call on Pastor Rooker When I arrived at the Baptist Church, Rooker was sitting at a picnic table near the parking lot thumbing through a Bible and making notes on a yellow legal pad. He motioned for me to join him.

"Good morning, Brother Logan. Good to see you. Everything going to suit you?" The man was bright and cheerful. His snow white hair and broad smile made him immediately likable. "It's been so hot I just decided to sit outside where it's cooler. Brother Bruce tells me you had a visit from Mrs. Irma and want to ask me some questions."

"Yes Sir, it's about a pamphlet." Just then I remembered I had left the pamphlet in Helm's office. "I'm sorry, Sir. I left it in Bruce's office. Let me go back and get..."

"Don't worry about it. I probably have a dozen of them in my office. Mrs. Irma leaves one on my car about every month or two. She's very dependable."

"You and Bruce both call her Mrs. Irma. It's like you know her."

"No, not really. She came to church here a time or two but somehow I heard she got hooked-up with one of those television preachers and I never saw her again. I guess she thinks she's doing God's work passing out those Bible tracts, but I can promise you, she's paying for them out of her own pocket and..."

"In other words, the only one coming out ahead is the guy printing the tracts."

"Exactly," responded Rooker. "Those tracts are amazing to me. There's not one word of truth in any of them and the guy has tracts on every religion, club and organization you can think of. I can't believe people would actually believe those things."

"In other words, there's nothing to worry about?"

"No. Not one thing. It's all absurd."

"But in the pamphlet says only the highest ranking Masons know about Baphomet."

Pastor Rooker reached over and shook my hand and as he did he turned my wrist and pointed to his ring. "Do you know what that is?" he asked.

"No Sir, a gold ring?"

"No, it's a bit more than that. Notice the 33 and three bands around it. It's a sign that I am a thirty-third Degree Mason. Last time I checked there wasn't anything higher. And, I can promise you that if there was any devil worship anywhere in Masonry I would have been out long ago. There's nothing to it. I promise you. By the way, I don't remember seeing you in church."

"No Sir, I'm an Episcopalian."

"Oh, one of Phil's boys."

"You know Father Byers?"

"Oh, Phil and I have played golf every Wednesday for as long as I can remember. I think the world of him, but Brother Bruce said you had another concern."

"Yes Sir, I do. The thing about the black Masons. Something just doesn't sound right."

"No, it doesn't sound right and it isn't right. But, my brother, that's just the way it is... at least in North Carolina. I think some of the New England states have changed it and maybe California, but my friend, it's going to be a long time before anyone in the south changes anything. For now, they're clandestine. You know what that means?" he asked.

"Yes Sir, in the obligation, we swore not to sit in a lodge with a clandestine Mason."

"That's right and you don't have to like it, but for now, if you want to be a Mason in North Carolina, you do have to live with it."

My visit to Rooker had cleared up some of my thoughts, but the answers still didn't seem right. In the lecture that followed my First Degree something had been said about Masonry looking at all men as equals. Obviously, that wasn't exactly true. If that wasn't true, what else in the myriad of books, booklets, lectures and lessons about Masonry wasn't true? Though we try to put things that make us uncomfortable out of our minds, enough small events occurred to not let me forget I was a member of a racist organization.

Yet, racist or not, there was much about Masonry I admired and came to love. I became very involved in my lodge, served in all the officer positions, including Master, And, when Pastor Rooker retired, I accepted the position of Secretary. Over the years, Masonry had become an important part of my life.

Each year, my Masonic Lodge sponsored a spaghetti supper for charity. Though we had an occasional black person attend, it was almost automatic that they would pick up a plate at the door and leave. But one particular year a thirtyish looking black man came in and went straight to the dining room. As soon as he took a seat, eyes darted among those serving plates.

"You gonna' to wait on the Nigger?" one of the guys whispered to me.

"Just wait a while," one of the others said in not too quiet voice. "He'll go up, get a plate and leave."

"Bullshit," I said as I picked up a plate, "his dollar's as good as the next. I'll wait on him."

It was almost fun glancing at the shocked faces as I headed toward the man.

"So, you're the one who's going to serve the Nigger," the man said as I sat his plate in front of him and aligned his silverware.

"'Nigger,' that's an unusual name. Is it your first name or last?

"Look dude, I can hear the word Nigger a mile away," said the man.

"That, my friend, is a valuable talent. Have you made the CIA aware? Might be big bucks," I retorted not to be outdone.

The man smiled. "Don't worry. I'll just eat and get out of here."

"No rush. You paid for it, enjoy it, but seriously, what is your name?" I asked.

"Mark..., Mark Avery. And yours?"

"David Logan. Glad you came and remember. It's all you can eat," I said. "You paid for it, if you want more just let me know. It's really pretty good. You'll probably want more. I'll check back with you later."

"Don't worry, everybody in this room is staring at me."

"Oh hell, they're just overprotective about the silverware."

He looked down at the spoon and knife, "they're just tin."

I smiled and said, "don't tell them, they think it's silver."

It would be six months before I would see Mark again. This time it would be at the Mall. I was in the Chik-fil-A when I heard someone ask, "can a darker brother sit with you?" I looked up and immediately recognized the man. "Mark Avery," I said.

"You remember my name"

"Sure I do, but I thought your taste was more toward spaghetti."

"No, actually I love these things, especially the waffle fries."

"Please, sit."

"I'm surprised you remember me."

"Why wouldn't I?" I asked. "Some people would've thought coming into the dining room that night would be a bit gutsy, but you did it anyhow."

"Yea, and you'll never know how much I appreciate how you treated me. I had to find out something."

"Find out something?" I asked not having any idea what he was talking about.

"Yea," he said as he shoved his hand toward the middle of the table. On his ring finger was a bright new Masonic ring.

"Am I noticing something new?" I asked smiling.

"I was Raised Tuesday night."

"Well congratulations. You're now a Master Mason. Proud of you, Brother."

"I think some would be a little sensitive about you calling me Brother."

"Yea, maybe so, but screw them. They have problems I don't have, but you still haven't answered me. You said you came that night because you had to find out something. What?"

"I've wanted to be a Mason all my life. My Grandfather was one and he was a wonderful man."

"Okay, but that still doesn't answer my question. Why did you come that night?"

"All my life I've heard that Masons are supposed to treat each other with respect. They're supposed to love each other."

"Okay," I responded. "They're supposed to."

"You also know that's a bunch of crap."

"What do you mean?" I asked.

"A black Mason may love and respect another black Mason and a white Mason may love and respect another white Mason, but it doesn't work all the way around. To most white Masons I'm just a Nigger and to most black Masons..."

"I'm just a Honkie," I said before Mark had a chance to say it.

"Yea... you're just a Honkie and I was told that if I went to that dinner and sat down I wouldn't find one Mason who would treat me as anything but a Nigger. So I went."

"Still why?"

"Because if there was one Mason who treated me as something more than..."

"Okay. I get your point, but what if the situation was reversed. What if I had gone to a black Masonic dinner?"

"You'd have been treated with respect, but it wouldn't be the respect of a fellow Mason. It would be the respect of someone who had been waiting on your kind for three hundred years."

"Well, what happened? What did you see?"

"Something better that I expected. I actually expected to be asked out."

"No, that wouldn't have happened."

"No, and only a couple of your guys even acted rude."

"You mean your supersonic nig-dar?"

"Yea, my supersonic nig-dar." He smiled. "But there's a few assholes in every group, Masons are no exception. I can accept that, but when you went out of your way to welcome me, even joke with me, then maybe there was something to this Masonic thing. Maybe there was hope. That night, after I left the spaghetti dinner I went to my Granddad's and told him I wanted to become a Mason. He beamed!"

"That is great, Mark"

"Yea, it is great, but one question... am I your brother? Seriously, am I really your brother?"

I looked straight into Mark's eyes. He was asking me a serious question, a question I had rather not answer. "Are you asking me, Mark, or are you asking the system? If you're asking me the answer is yes... hell yes! But if you're asking some archaic system set up two centuries ago by a

bunch of holier than thou slave owners and perpetuated by a
bunch of insecure Rednecks, I would have to say no."

Chapter 3

1977

In 1997 I was appointed to the Grand Lodge Committee on Research and Development. For years, such appointments were little more than a political "thank you" given by a Grand Master during his year to a friend. With rare exception, most of the committees did little, and even less was expected. I didn't know this and grabbed my new position with gusto.

The committee met in Raleigh about once a month and I was in awe of the others who were members. Many were men I had never met, but whose names I had seen constantly in Masonic publications through the previous years. Some could be defined as the movers and shakers of Masonry in North Carolina. I often felt overwhelmed.

As the year progressed, I became close to several on the committee, one especially, a Presbyterian minister from the mountains. I found Ralph Moss to be one of the kindest, most sincere people I had ever met. He never said anything unkind about anyone or complained about anything. All that year the committee worked in perfect unison and produced study materials for the over three hundred lodges like they had never seen before. Anything that was asked of the committee was produced and anything the committee asked of the Grand Lodge was granted. Everything appeared in perfect harmony... at least with the committee. Elsewhere, my old-time fly in the ointment, the race issue, was about to surface.

The "Hallmart Moment" came in the spring when a young military man from California visited a lodge near Camp Lejune, a large Marine Corps. Base. Since the Grand

Lodge California is recognized as a regular Grand Lodge by the Grand Lodge of North Carolina, the man should have been admitted without incident. His visit should have been business as usual, but there was a problem. The man was black. As rightfully should have been done for any member of a recognized Grand Lodge, the Master allowed the man to be seated. But, rather than sit with a Black man, several of the members walked out refusing to sit with a Black. The members who walked out made no secret that their rationale for leaving was the man's race. The fact that the Master refused to side with the members immediately brought the matter to the attention of the Grand Master Glenn Sands.

Sands was a gentle man who would have rather avoided such confrontation, but his hand was forced by the issue and when he realized the unmasonic nature of what had happened, he supported the stand of the Master of the lodge. Talk of the event spread through the fraternity, but the end result would not be seen until it came to a head in July.

A small war ensued for several months. I heard about the event when I was in Raleigh for a meeting, but for the average member heard nothing not until July.

An article appeared in the July issue of the *N.C. Mason*,

the fraternity's newspaper. The Board of General Purposes, the Grand Master's advisory board, unanimously voted for a resolution that condemned racism. The article drew comments as few articles in the past had done before.

IN THE NEWS

North Carolina Mason July/August 1997

Resolution Of The Board Of General Purposes Grand Lodge Of Ancient, Free And Accepted Masons Of North Carolina

WHEREAS, racial discrimination is abhorrent and unacceptable, and

WHEREAS, Freemasonry and the Grand Lodge of North Carolina teach the principles of friendship, morality, and brotherly love, and

WHEREAS, Freemasonry regards the internal and not the external qualifications of a man, and

WHEREAS, the right of visitation is a Masonic landmark recognized in this Grand Jurisdiction,

NOW THEREFORE, THE BOARD OF GENERAL PURPOSES OF THE GRAND LODGE OF ANCIENT, FREE AND ACCEPTED MASONS OF NORTH CAROLINA

RESOLVES that racial discrimination is abhorrent, unacceptable, and unmasonic.

BE IT FURTHER RESOLVED that no board, committee, commission, subordinate lodge, or associated Masonic body in this Grand Jurisdiction shall maintain any racially discriminatory guidelines, practices, or policies.

BE IT FURTHER RESOLVED that the master of a Masonic lodge in this Grand Jurisdiction shall not consider the race of any Brother from a recognized lodge in deciding who may visit in my lodge.

BE IT FURTHER RESOLVED that the master of a Masonic lodge in this Grand Jurisdiction shall not consider any objection to such a visitation that he believes is based on race.

Unanimously adopted this 20th day of June, 1997 by the members here present:

My lodge holds two meetings a month and at the second meeting a dinner is served. It's a wonderful social opportunity for the brothers with open conversation on every subject conceivable.

Brother Albert Williams mentioned the article at the first lodge dinner after it appeared. "Brothers," he announced to everyone in earshot, "did anyone see that thing in the *N.C. Mason* about racism? I can't believe those people did that."

Tallon Trask piped in by asking, "you mean what that board did?"

"Yea, that thing about we're supposed to go along with those Niggers calling themselves Masons. That ain't what I learned. I was told ain't no Niggers can be no Mason."

All of a sudden, the entire table seemed interested.

Another person piped in, "Didn't make any sense to me either. Colored Masons are clandestine. We swore not to have anything to do with 'em. It's right there in our oath."

"Yea, you exactly right and I hear that two Niggers already tried to get into a couple of lodges and they kicked 'em out," said Trask.

"That's what they supposed to do," said Mark Simpson. "They're clandestine."

I began speaking before I had considered my actions. "It wasn't in that article, but somewhere in the paper it said that several grand lodges have already recognized Prince Hall Masons."

"How can they do that?" asked Trask. "They're clandestine. Everybody knows that."

"Yea," said someone else. "I guarantee you it's them damn Yankee grand lodges. They think Niggers is just like white folks."

"Maybe so," I said, "but it wasn't two black guys you were talking about, it was one. And, he was from a Grand Lodge we recognize. Far as our Grand Lodge is concerned, he is a real Mason. A Mason just like us."

"Maybe we recognized them,"said Trask, "whatever the hell that means, but my coach told me no Nigger could ever be a Mason and my coach was one of the smartest Masons I ever knew. He knew what he was talking about."

"Evidently not," I said, "not if we recognize them."

"Even if they're Niggers?" asked Trask getting somewhat excited..

"What's that got to do with it?" I asked.

Barry Welch, who hadn't said anything spoke up, "who let this damn Nigger lover in?" he asked looking directly at me.

"You can call me a Nigger lover if you want to, but I'm just trying to tell you the way it is."

Tom Lang motioned to say something. "You keep talking about this recognizing stuff. What do you mean by recognized?"

"It means we recognize, we accept, them as Masons, just as much a Mason as any one of us."

"Can we do that? I thought Niggers couldn't be Masons, period."

"The Grand Lodge recognizes other grand lodges every year. Last year we recognized the Bahamas and Liberia. They are Black and any one of their members can walk into one of our lodges and we're supposed to accept them. If we don't it's wrong."

"It won't wrong if it's a damn Nigger," said someone at the end of the table. "They can't be Masons."

"If you people don't mind, I wish you'd quit saying 'Nigger'. It makes you sound so stupid and I'm not going to argue with you. You brought it up. I didn't."

"Sorry if I offend you, brother," Trask seemed to strain on the word brother, "but that's the way I was brought up."

"Well, I can promise you, you're going to see a whole lot more of it before it's all over."

"God, I hope not," said Trask as he walked out.

I was surprised that Williams and Trask only noticed the article about the Board of General Purposes resolution. Because in the same paper there was an article by the Grand Master, Glenn Sands, in which he said:

> "...Another place we must show our leadership is in encouraging the right of visitation of a Brother who holds a valid dues card from a lodge recognized by our jurisdiction.

In the past, a few of our members have discouraged
or prevented Masons from visiting their lodges
because they didn't like the race, looks, or
nationality of the visitor.

This is not Masonic and has no place in Masonry.
We must show our respect for the work we do and
that holy book upon the altar. We must each show
Masonic leadership toward doing what is right. We
may otherwise lose opportunities to meet some very
interesting Brothers and a view of Masonry in other
parts of our world. We may also hurt our public
image and give anti-Masons ammunition with which
to attack. Masonry teaches brotherly love and
toleration. Now let's practice those lessons in our
daily lives."

In the very same issue, the Editor of the *NC Mason*
wrote an editorial entitled "It's Time to Stand Up". The
editorial concluded:

"A Mason's stand against racism is simple. Anyone
who has taken the degrees of Masonry and read the
Holy Bible knows in his breast what is right — Every
Mason must judge a man by what is in the heart, not

by what is on his flesh.

If you've stopped being part of your lodge because of perceived intolerance, it's time for you to return. It's time for all good Masons — believers in brotherly love — to step forward and exert their influence in their home lodge. It's time for each of us to speak up for what's right.

If you're uncomfortable with The Resolution, you should give yourself and Freemasonry an opportunity to reach for the horizon. You may well find new avenues in new experiences.

It will take fortitude, but our leaders are leading, and now it's our turn to do what we can to help show the world that Freemasonry in North Carolina stands against racism."

It was certain that things were happening.

That night during the meeting itself, I kept rethinking the events at dinner. It wasn't what Williams or Trask had said. They were racists and proud of it. It was those who had said nothing that I was contemplating. I had to wonder exactly what was coming. And, I wondered what was going on in the minds of those I call "brother."

Chapter 4

1998

The next few months were calm. Little was mentioned about race, bigotry or even Prince Hall. I heard Trask tell someone that it was just somebody making noise and it was like a cat crap, if we don't stir it, it will go away. I wouldn't have to wait long to see the membership's attitude about the resolution by the Board of General Purposes. In April of 1998 at the annual meeting, the delegates refused to support the resolution. In a heated discussion, the ins and outs of the resolution became a quagmire that eventually resulted in no vote. Those who had sworn to uphold the equality of man had refused to uphold the equality of the races. Yet, at the conclusion of the session, in his last action as Grand Master, outgoing Grand

Master Sands dropped a bombshell that would rock the fraternity for more than a decade. He announced that he was forming a task force to study the recognition of The Most Worshipful Prince Hall Grand Lodge of Free and Accepted Masons of North Carolina... the black Masons. In a memorable speech, he stated that the reason was simple... "it was the right thing to do".

I was sitting with Ralph Moss as the Grand Master made his speech and when he announced that the chairman of the committee would be Ralph Moss, My head snapped to my left. "Did you know about this?" I asked.

"Of course I did," answered Moss.

"Well then, I've got to ask. Are you out of your mind?"

"Why?" asked Moss in obvious surprise.

"Ralph, I would be surprised if there isn't a crowd headed out to cut the tires on your car right now. Where were you when all these good people of yours wouldn't even approve the BGP anti-racism resolution?"

"I think that one just caught them off guard. No, Logan, these people are Masons. They don't think that way."

"Bless you Ralph," I thought, "I wish you
but I know you are wrong."

Word of the Grand Master's action spread through th
membership at an unbelievable rate. The next morning I
joined my friends at Bojangles for our regular breakfast
get-together.

"I got a call last night," said Allen Marks. "Someone
tells me we're getting ready to merge with the Niggers.
Stupidest thing I ever heard of."

"No, you heard wrong," I responded in a curt manner,
"nobody has said anything about merging with anyone. All
the Grand Master did was appoint a group to study
recognizing Prince Hall Masonry. That's all. No one has said
a thing about merging."

"What do you mean recognizing?"

"Just saying they are Masons just like us. We just
'recognize' their Masonry. It's no big deal." God, I was
getting tired of repeating that. It was hard for me to believe
these people had been Masons for years and didn't even
know what "recognize" means.

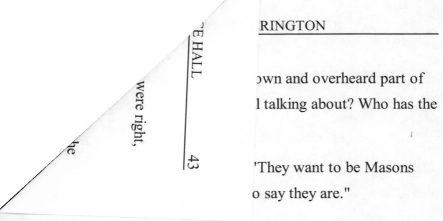

)wn and overheard part of
l talking about? Who has the

'They want to be Masons
o say they are."

"How can we do that? Asked Barry, "they're not.
They're not real Masons. They just call themselves that.
Now they want us to say they're just like us. What else do
those damn people want?"

I rolled my eyes. "They don't want a damn thing," I
said. "The Grand Master just said that they are there. They
are Masons just like us and it is time for us to quit
pretending they don't exist."

"I don't get what you're saying, Logan. We all know
they're not real Masons. That was one of the first things
they told me... Niggers can't be real Masons. How can they
be like us? They don't even do the same stuff. We don't
even know if they say the same..." Barry clicked his fingers
trying to remember the word.

Allen chimed in, "ritual."

"Yea, ritual. We don't even know what their ritual says."

"Good God," I said. "That's why the Grand Master appointed the committee. To study those things and find out. No one's saying we do a thing until all those questions are answered. That's as far as it goes. He just wants us to study it. Then... depending on what they find, that's when we do something... or don't. Like I say, depending on what they find."

Barry nodded his head then asked, "why, after all these years, have the Niggers just now decided to ask us to..." he clicked his fingers again.

"Recognize them," I said.

"Yea, recognize them. Why after all this time are the Niggers all of a sudden asking us to.. recognize them."

"Barry, would you quit saying 'Niggers'? It makes you sound so goddamn stupid."

"Well, I don't like it when you say GD."

"I know. That's exactly why I said it. You don't like 'GD' and I don't like 'Niggers'."

"Yea, but it's a sin to use God's name in vain."

"To me, it's a sin to sound stupid. So, let's both not do it."

"Okay, but answer my question. Why, all of a sudden are the Nigg... pardon me, the Negroes, asking us to do... that thing?"

"I think they like 'Blacks', but I don't know that they've asked for anything. The Grand Master said we are doing it because it's the right thing to do. Not because they asked."

"Gezzus," said Allen. "The Grand Master is a white man. Isn't he?"

I nodded my head.

"Why would a white man, any white man, out of the blue, ask us to recognize a bunch of..." Allen smiled at me, "...Blacks... that haven't even asked? Doesn't make sense. You can say what you want to, but it's just like everything else. We let 'em in our schools... the schools have gone to hell. We let 'em in our neighborhoods... they're ain't a white neighborhood left. We do this recognizing thing and before long they'll be taking over our lodges. It just ain't right.""

"Well, the Grand Master says it's the right thing to do. And, I agree with him."

"Right thing or not right thing," said Barry, "you know as well as I do, when it comes down to a vote, ain't no white man in this state gonna' vote to let in no Nigg.. Black. Just ain't gonna' happen."

"No one is asking to let them in our lodges or anything else. They're just wanting to study the right thing to do."

"That's how it always starts, but if we get to vote... well, like I said. It just ain't gonna' happen."

"I don't know," I said as I asked about the upcoming NC State - Duke game. I couldn't do anything but fear that maybe Barry knew what he was talking about. Right or wrong may have nothing to do with it.

The next few months were quiet. Very quiet. A comment was made every now and then but it appeared that if the subject of recognizing Prince Hall wasn't mentioned, it might just go away.

A new Grand Master, Ted Green, took office. As had been done in the past, the new Grand Master, a mild-mannered businessman from the western part of the state, began conducting District Meetings. At each one, he made it clear that the Prince Hall Recognition study would be at the top of his agenda. At each one, he encountered opposition. Yet, he was obviously committed to the belief that it was the right thing.

The new Grand Master began his tenure with an item in the *NC Mason* which read, in part:

> "I intend not to sweep the topic of hatred and bigotry under the carpet. I plan to speak against intolerance and racism as long as I am your Grand Master. I will do that with whatever few talents I possess. I know that the measure of a man has nothing to do with his race. I know that if there is a Masonic Lodge in Heaven, it most certainly has good men of every color seated in it, and I believe the Great Architect of the Universe would consider no objection based on the color of a man's skin.
>
> Masonry teaches us that we are all children of one almighty parent — that we are to aid, support, and

protect each other — that it is the internal and not the external qualifications of a man that should recommend him to be made a Mason — that Masonry unites men of every country, sect, and opinion, and conciliates true friendship among those who otherwise would have remained at a perpetual distance.

Elbert White was My Masonic catechism coach many years ago. As good coaches always do, he taught me about more than just the ritual. He helped children throughout our city. There's no telling how many pairs of shoes he bought for needy children.

There's no counting the number of bats, balls, and gloves he gave to children whose families could not afford them. He was colorblind to the color of a person's skin — he just saw someone in need.

We were returning from a Masonic funeral when we last discussed the issue of race. He said that bigots are like the pupil of your eye — the more light you put on them, the more they shrink away.

Well brethren, I plan to put as much Masonic light on that topic as I can this year. I know that upsets some of you. I can't help that. Like you, I was first made a Mason in my heart, and my heart says love your neighbor as yourself.

The Grand Lodge of North Carolina will never realize it's potential until it deals effectually with the issue of race.

A black Mason from a lodge recognized by our Grand Lodge has every right to visit a lodge here in North Carolina. As Grand Master, I will not tolerate a situation where this man is turned away because of the color of his skin.

Someone at Annual Communication said we shouldn't air our dirty laundry. No brethren, we shouldn't air it — we should wash it! With our prayers and the blessing of God, we can all do the right thing. We only have to look at our Masonic teaching and be attentive to what we feel in our hearts. I have every confidence that the Masons of this state will do just that.

In July 1998, I met with the Education Committee in Raleigh at the monthly meeting. While I was there, I chanced to run into Ralph Moss.

As we met, I showed my joy in seeing my old friend. "You know I wish you were still on the Education Committee," I said meaning every word.

"You got to admit, we did do good for a while didn't we?" Ralph said through a broad smile.

"Yes we did. How's the new committee going? The Grand Master's District meetings aren't making him a loved one in the camp," I said.

"Oh, he can handle it," said Ralph. "It's just a few loudmouths trying to hold onto the way it was. They'll calm down soon enough. We're scheduling the listening sessions now. That'll give them a chance to vent. Then, they should be okay."

"Listening sessions," I asked. "What do you mean by listening sessions?"

"The Task Force is scheduling listening sessions around the state. We figure that when all the opinions are in, the

Masons will do the right thing. This way, when recognition passes, no one can say that we didn't ask."

I suddenly felt weak. I couldn't believe what he was saying. "Ralph, are you serious? Do you realize how hostile these people actually are?"

"Oh, some of them from down your way are, but the most of our guys are decent Masons. They'll live up to their obligations. I have faith in them."

"Ralph, I gotta' ask you. Are all Presbyterians as stupid as you are?"

Ralph chuckled. "David, you've just been listening to the wrong people. They'll come across. Just wait and see."

I half-way stuttered. "Ralph, I didn't mean to call you stupid. Naive is maybe a better word, but you can't be serious about having listening sessions."

"Dead serious. The letter is going out as we speak. They start in September, that's why I'm in Raleigh today."

"Ralph, I take back what I said. You are stupid."

"Just wait, my friend. You'll see. You'll see."

IN THE NEWS

North Carolina Mason July/August 1998

Prince Hall Task Force To Hold Listening Meetings

The Grand Lodge Task Force created to investigate Prince Hall recognition in North Carolina will be holding "active listening" sessions at ten locations around the state in September.

Each lodge will give a three-minute position statement to be put on permanent, published record to aid the Craft in its 1999 decision. Begin work now to make a lodge statement you can be proud of. Lodges will be notified as soon as the final schedule is available. Ask your secretary or DDGM.

Few Masonic meetings are ever well-attended, but Ralph Moss's "Listening Sessions" were a gross exception. I made a point of attending the first session. From the very start, the comments were ugly... very ugly. At the first session one speaker stood and made no effort to hide his feelings. "I have been a Mason for over forty years and was told from the very start that those people are clandestine. I wasn't even supposed to talk to them, least not about Masonry. Now we're supposed to throw the doors wide open to them. Don't make one bit of sense."

Before he could be seated another man stood and said, "I was told them Niggers can't be Masons. They just say they're Masons. Do you people know what the hell you're doing? This is the stupidest thing I ever heard of. The Niggers have taken every other damn thing from the whites. They've screwed up our schools. Half the son-of-a-bitches are on welfare and I..."

The man in charge interrupted the speaker, "Brother... brother... we're not going to lose our tempers. I can see..."

The speaker immediately retorted. "Wait just a damn minute. You people asked for our opinion and now you're telling me I can't say what I want. I have the floor and as I was saying... half of those black son-of-a-bitches are on welfare and..."

The man at the front slammed down a gavel and said, "Brother... maybe I didn't say it so you could understand it. I'll try again. I know some of you are angry that this subject even came up, but even so, we are going to conduct ourselves as Masons and gentlemen and if you can't do that you will not be allowed to speak. Yes, Brother, we want your opinion, but there's a right way and a wrong way and for one thing, the people we're talking about are Prince Hall Masons, not Niggers. Now, Brother, if you think you can conduct yourself in a civil manner, we'll hear what you have to say."

"Excuse me, Bother," said the man speaking, "I apologize for my way of talking and it won't happen again. But what I was saying is the Nigg... excuse me, the blacks.. ain't real Masons. I was told that from the very start. If I'd have thought for one minute that I was going to have to socialize with some... black, I wouldn't be here. I wouldn't want to be here."

Each speaker had been given three minutes to present his thoughts. For the remaining two minutes the speaker basically repeated himself. The following two speakers said the same. Then, another speaker stood. "Do we even know what ritual them Prince Hall people use? Ain't none of us ever seen their ritual. Do they use the same ritual we do? Does anybody know?"

Even the man in charge was taken aback by the question but his response was good. "I can't answer your question,

Brother, but that's why the Grand Master formed the task force, to look into things exactly like what you're asking."

To put into its simplest terms, the "Listening Sessions" were a disaster. The "kind", "gentle" Masons from whom Ralph Moss expected hear, if they existed at all... were few. Though there were several who spoke for recognition, and spoke eloquently, from the first, most of the reports, discussion and statements were the racist South at its worst.

Comments ranged from complex doubts about the "regularity" of Prince Hall Masonry to simple "I ain't gonna' sit in no lodge with a Nigger." Others stood religiously by the "Code", a book of rules and regulations. In the Code it states that the Grand Lodge of North Carolina is the only governing Masonic body in the state and no other Masonic entity shall be recognized. To some, the statement seemed iron-clad and irrefutable. It seemed iron-clad until someone realized it had no legal authority over anyone but the present members.

Masonry has a complex system of one "body" must originate from another. The system has gone on for centuries. As far as Masonry is concerned, anything created on its own has no merit, and for all intents and purposes, doesn't exist. The holy grail of this heritage is the Grand Lodge of England which was established in 1717. To the many of the Grand Lodges, any Masonic group that cannot trace its ancestry back to the Grand Lodge of England is simply not there. Members of such groups, though they may call themselves Masons, are not allowed into mainstream lodges. We are not allowed to discuss Masonry in any form with them and they are not "real" Masons. The term "clandestine" is used to describe such people.

As soon as the listening sessions began, Masons who had never heard more than a casual mention of the Grand Lodge of England, and even then couldn't have cared less, were suddenly concerned with the Grand Lodge of England and Prince Hall Masonry's lineage to it. To some, it appeared impossible that an august body such as the Grand Lodge of England would have any connection with a group of blacks across the Atlantic. This doubt became certainty and an all-out effort developed to brush aside any talk of recognizing this "clandestine" bunch, Those against recognition rallied behind their new battle flag.

I had gotten to the lodge early and was sitting in my car

waiting for someone to open the door when a car pulled in beside me. It was Lem Tate, a grey haired man about sixty who had just retired from the railroad. As soon as he parked he jumped into my car. "Have you heard about all that's going on?" he asked.

I knew what he meant but decided to act as if I didn't. "What are you talking about?"

"That crowd in Raleigh is getting ready to throw the doors open to the Coloreds. I'm surprised you don't know anything about it."

"Oh, you're talking about Prince Hall recognition. Yea, I was there when the Grand Master announced it. I know about that."

"Well, way I understand it, they had a meeting in New Bern last week and those boys gave them a piece of their minds. Told 'em how stupid the whole idea was. I can't believe they even brought it up."

"I really don't see what's the big deal. All they're wanting to do is recognize them," I said.

"I don't know where you got your information but

that's not what I heard. Way I heard it, they want us to merge with 'em. Want us to take 'em in like real Masons. My god. I can't believe they're even asking us for such a thing. Them people ain't even real Masons. They're clandestine. I don't know about you, but I swore an oath not to have anything to do with nobody clandestine. I ain't breaking my oath for nobody, 'specially that crowd in Raleigh."

"Lem, Lem, Lem, cool your jets. No one is asking anyone to merge with anybody. No one is asking for anything but to recognize them."

"Well, what the hell you think recognize means?"

"The same thing it always has. It just to say we accept them as Masons... not one thing more. Not a Grand Lodge session has gone by that we didn't recognize somebody. It's done every session. It's no big thing."

"David, we're talking about Coloreds."

I chuckled. "Lem, what do you think is in the Bahamas, and Kenya, and half the countries in Africa?"

"Colored people, I guess, but what's that got to do with

anything?"

"We have recognized half of them. And, they got full recognition. Any one of those guys from the Bahamas or Africa can walk into any one of our lodges and be legal."

"I didn't know that, but it don't matter. Those places are a thousand miles away. Ain't none of them coming here to go to no lodge. Them Prince Halls are right here. They can walk in any time if we let 'em. It ain't the same."

"You're barking up the wrong tree. Nobody's asking for visitation. All anybody wants to do is recognize them. Like I said, it's no big deal."

I knew he was wrong, but for some of the Masons it was a big deal. It would mark the end of the largest all-white organization in North Carolina. It was becoming even clearer than I had imagined, and those against it weren't going to take it laying down.

The two of us sat there for a while and talked about Duke and Carolina, but my mind wasn't on college teams, I was wondering how long I wanted to stay a member of a lodge that each day seemed more like a Klan Klavern.

As 1998 progressed, the animosity between those supporting recognition of Prince Hall Masonry and those against grew. Letters were sent to and published in the *North Carolina Mason* and the Tarheel Mason's list on the Internet became totally hostile with name calling of every form and description. The recognition issue had been called divisive, and it was living up to its reputation.

Letters, Internet posts and conversations flew about the pending legislation. Some bordered on hate as is seen in this letter to the North Carolina Mason.

MOST WORSHIPFUL BROTHER YOU STATED THAT YOU "WILL NOT TOLERATE" SITUATIONS THAT YOU EQUATE WITH RACISM. YET THE CODE OF THE GRAND LODGE OF North Carolina CLEARLY STATES, " IT MUST BE LEFT WITH THE MEMBERS OF THE CRAFT TO DETERMINE WHETHER OR NOT... A BROTHER IS BRING REPROACH UPON MASONRY BY HIS CONDUCT, AND THEREBY IS, OR IS NOT, GUILTY OF UNMASONIC CONDUCT. A MASONIC OFFENSE IS... A VIOLATION OF THE LAWS, USAGES, AND CUSTOMS OF MASONRY.

MOST WORSHIPFUL BROTHER HAS NO AUTHORITY WHATSOEVER TO DECIDE WHAT WILL OR WILL NOT BE TOLERATED IN THE LODGES OF NORTH CAROLINA,

SO LONG AS THE PRACTICES OF A LODGE CONFORMS TO THE ANCIENT LANDMARKS OF MASONRY AND THE LAWS, USAGES AND CUSTOMS OF MASONRY. IT APPEARS THAT BROTHER WISHES TO CHANGE THE ANCIENT CUSTOMS OF MASONRY, BUT DOESN'T HAVE THE INTEGRITY OR THE COURAGE TO SAY SO OPENLY. INSTEAD,

HE TRIES TO MAKE US FEEL GUILTY FOR CONTINUING TO PRACTICE MASONRY AS WE ALWAYS HAVE. WHAT IS THE DIFFERENCE BETWEEN VIOLATING THOSE LAWS, USAGES, AND CUSTOMS ONESELF, AND ATTEMPTING TO PERSUADE THE ENTIRE GRAND LODGE OF NORTH CAROLINA TO VIOLATE THEM?

MOST WORSHIPFUL BROTHER ALSO STATES THAT "A BLACK MASON FROM A LODGE RECOGNIZED BY OUR GRAND LODGE HAS EVERY RIGHT TO VISIT A LODGE HERE IN NORTH CAROLINA". YES, HE DOES - UNLESS

A MEMBER OBJECTS. THE CODE CLEARLY
STATES THAT A MEMBER OF A LODGE HAS
A RIGHT TO OBJECT TO THE PRESENCE OR
THE ADMISSION OF A VISITING MASON,
THAT THIS IS A PERSONAL RIGHT AND MAY
BE COMMUNICATED PRIVATELY TO THE
MASTER OF THAT LODGE, THAT THE
MASTER SHOULD GIVE PREFERENCE IN
THIS MATTER TO THE WISHES OF THE
MEMBER OVER THE WISHES OF A VISITING
MASON, THAT THE VISITOR CANNOT AS A
RIGHT DEMAND THE NAME OF THE
OBJECTOR OR THE GROUNDS OF HIS
OBJECTION, AND THAT EVEN THE MASTER
OF THE LODGE CANNOT REQUIRE THE
MEMBER TO GIVE HIS REASONS FOR
OBJECTING TO THE PRESENCE OF A
VISITING MASON, NOR MAY THE MEMBER
BE DISCIPLINED FOR OBJECTING. THE CODE
MAKES NO PROVISION WHATSOEVER FOR A
GRAND MASTER TO JUDGE A BROTHER
MASON IN THIS MATTER, OR FOR A GRAND
MASTER TO DECIDE FOR HIMSELF WHAT
THE MEMBER'S REASONS ARE. SINCE THE
CODE FORBIDS THE GRAND MASTER FROM
QUESTIONING THE MEMBERS WHO'S VOTES
AND OBJECTIONS HE DOESN'T LIKE, HE
GUESSES AT SOMETHING HE HAS NO WAY
OF KNOWING ABOUT. AND NO WAY AS A

MASON, OR AS A GRAND MASTER TO OBJECT TO, AND CAUSES HIS GUESSES TO BE PUBLISHED IN THE NORTH CAROLINA MASON. CONFIDENTIALITY, SECRECY, AND SELF-DETERMINATION ARE IMPORTANT PARTS OF MASONRY. REGARDING CONFIDENTIALITY AND SELF DETERMINATION IN SECRET BALLOTS THE CODE SAYS, "THE INTENTION OF THIS REGULATION IS TO PRESERVE TO THE LODGE AND THE CRAFT THE FULL BENEFITS OF A SECRET BALLOT. EACH MEMBER VOTING IS THE SOLE JUDGE OF WHAT HIS VOTE SHALL BE, AND HE SHALL NOT BE QUESTIONED THEREFOR OR ON ACCOUNT THEREOF."

CLEARLY, THIS IS THE REAL HEART OF THE MATTER: MOST WORSHIPFUL BROTHER WANTS MORE POWER OVER HIS BROTHER MASONS, AND HE IS WILLING TO VIOLATE THE CODE, CONSTITUTION, AND RIGHTS OF EVERY MASON, TO CAUSE DISHARMONY, ENCOURAGE CONTROVERSY, AND EVEN COMMIT MASONIC OFFENSES TO OBTAIN THAT POWER. WHEN A BROTHER IS WILLING TO IGNORE THE LAWS, USAGES, AND CUSTOMS OF MASONRY, AND CAUSE DISHARMONY AND CONTROVERSY WITHIN THE CRAFT AS WELL, IS HE REALLY A

MASON?

IF I CALL MYSELF A HINDU BUT EAT ROAST BEEF EVERY SUNDAY AND ENCOURAGE OTHER HINDUS TO DO SO, AM I REALLY A HINDU? IF I CALL MYSELF A DALLAS COWBOY BUT GIVE THE BALL TO A PITTSBURG STEELER IN A GAME, AM I REALLY A DALLAS COWBOY?

NOT FOR LONG, YOU CAN BET. MOST WORSHIPFUL BROTHER STATES THAT HE "WAS FIRST MADE A MASON IN HIS HEART", AND SOME OF US WONDER WHEN HE HAD HIS MASONIC HEART REPLACED WITH A PROFANE HEART. IF WE ALLOW THE GRAND MASTER TO THROW AWAY THIS MASONIC LAW, WHAT WILL

HE TRY NEXT? SHALL WE THEN ADMIT WOMEN INTO THE LODGE? I'M SURE THAT THE GREAT ARCHITECT OF THE UNIVERSE WOULD CONSIDER NO OBJECTION BASED ON SEX. JESUS TOLD THE PHARISEES THAT THIEVES AND PROSTITUTES WOULD GET INTO THE KINDOM OF HEAVEN BEFORE THE PHARISEES WOULD. SHALL WE ADMIT THIEVES AND PROSTITUTES INTO THE LODGES? EITHER A MAN ACCEPTS THE ANCIENT AND ACCEPTED PRACTICES AND CUSTOMS OF MASONRY OR HE DOESN'T.

LETS NOT PRACTICE DECEIT WITH EACH
OTHER BROTHERS. A MAN OF INTEGRITY
WILL EITHER ACCEPT THE LAWS AND
CUSTOMS OF MASONRY, OR HE NEEDS TO
ADMIT THAT HE DOES NOT ACCEPT THEM
AND HE SHOULD THEN GET OUT OF THE
CRAFT!

By Brother Allen James

.

Such letters became common. In a discussion forum on
the Internet names, accusations, and outward hostility flew.
Brothers threatened resignation almost daily. Unsigned posts
became unbelievably hostile until the moderator banned
them and refused to allow any unsigned posts to be
published. Name calling became common in the lodges and
numerous officers who had spent years progressing through
the offices of the lodges lost elections because of simple
comments they made indicating they might be in favor of
recognition.

As with the other Grand Masters, the present Grand
Master went throughout the state holding his district
meetings. I attended two of these meetings and gained an
admiration for him like few I have ever known. In the

meetings, he was bombarded with comments worthy of the worst Mississippi Klu Klux Klan rally. For a man who established his conviction early and at every possible time, the comments were made to hurt. "I've known Niggers all my life and I ain't never known one..." was the type comments he would hear. "It's been proven that..." followed by some comment only the most ignorant bigot could believe, was common. Yet, with such comments flying, Grand Master Green would give full attention to the speaker acting as if he were listening to every sentence, every word. To this day I have to wonder what the man was thinking while the lowest element of our fraternity spewed their hate. Eventually, I had to ask him and his response once more made me proud to be a Mason.

He said "When I looked in the eyes of my Brothers as they made those comments, I saw myself as I used to be. I grew up thinking I was better than the black people in my community - smarter, better looking, and deserving of the privilege I enjoyed as a white person. In my twenties, when I joined the Fraternity, I began to try to be the best man I could be, and understanding the Brotherhood of man under the Fatherhood of God helped me deal with my bigotry. So I could only feel sorry for those men as although they were members of a Masonic Lodge, they were not yet Masons."

As 1998 came to a close, the Grand Lodge Committee on Masonic Education published almost a full page of questions and answers about Prince Hall Masonry. It was the hope of those on the committee that seeing the questions and answers in print would clear, at least, some of the air.

IN THE NEWS

North Carolina Mason   July/August 1998

The Grand Master has brought to the attention of the Committee on Masonic Education that information is sorely needed by the membership to review in determining their answer regarding the proposed amendment to recognize the Prince Hall Grand Lodge. Please share this with your members. The enclosed material DOES NOT take a position for or against the proposal, rather it provides some answers to some common questions about Prince Hall Masonry in order that the Craft may make a more informed decision. The decision to recognize any other Masonic body needs to be based on facts.

As you likely know, the Prince Hall Task Force (PHTF) has been holding listening sessions in September at regional locations to gather information on the concerns and feelings of all the lodges regarding this issue. It is also our understanding that PHTF will provide additional information following these sessions and a recommendation prior to the Annual Communication in April.

1. Where did Prince Hall Masonry come from?

A full history of Prince Hall Masonry is outside the scope of this brief pamphlet, but will be better addressed in a later communication from this committee or the Prince Hall Task Force.

Briefly, Prince Hall was a free black man who, along with 14 other black men in Boston, was initiated by a British army lodge in 1774. They were given permission to meet as African Lodge 459 by the Grand Lodge of England. Over time, the men lost touch with their grand lodge and began, as many other Masonic bodies of the time (including lodges in North Carolina) to practice

their Craft without benefit of grand lodge affiliation.

They were contacted by other black free citizens of

the time who wished to be Masons. Prince Hall and his

Masonic Brothers extended their knowledge to other

states outside Massachusetts. They eventually gathered

as a group and formed their own grand lodges.

The Prince Hall Grand Lodge of North Carolina,

chartered in 1870, is descended from these bodies.

2. Has the Prince Hall Grand Lodge asked for

recognition?

No. The national trend toward recognizing Prince

Hall Grand Lodges is widely known. In 1990 the Grand

Lodge of Connecticut recognized their resident Prince

Hall counterpart. Other states began to follow suit. In

1996, after lengthy investigation and consideration, the

United Grand Lodge of England pronounced Prince Hall

Masonry regular. Since 1990, 28 United States and most

Canadian Provinces have granted some form of recognition

to Prince Hall grand lodges in their jurisdiction.

Most of the recognitions are full and unconditional. The

progression made it a natural topic among Masons in

North Carolina.

3. Why is the recognition of Prince Hall being considered

by our Grand Lodge?

A proposal was submitted by Hominy 491 of Candler.

They were joined by Hiram 40 of Raleigh and

Doric 568 of New Bern. Any proposal submitted by a

subordinate lodge must be considered at the next Annual

Communication.

4. If approved will they become a part of the Grand Lodge

of North Carolina?

No. They would have no more influence than any

other grand jurisdiction we recognize.

5. What relationship will they have with our charities?

None. The rules for recommending a resident at our homes in Greensboro or Oxford will not change. Only a lodge operating under the Grand Lodge of North Carolina can make such a recommendation. For example, a Mason from the Grand Lodge of South Carolina residing in this state is not eligible to enter our Masonic and Eastern Star Home. Nor would a member of Prince Hall Grand Lodge be eligible. Neither would we gain any control of their charities.

6. Are we merging with Prince Hall?

No. If recognition is extended and reciprocated, then it is like the recognition given to, for example, the Grand Lodge of Virginia. Both the Prince Hall Grand Lodge and our Grand Lodge would remain sovereign over the lodges each maintains in our state.

7. Is Prince Hall Masonry regular or clandestine?

Clandestine and regular are terms long bandied

about by academics and legal minds. They will argue

the definitions of these terms for ages to come. In the

real world clandestine means unrecognized, recognized

means regular. Having fraternal relations makes

a grand lodge regular.

In your obligation, you made promises about discussions

you may have with clandestine Masons. Your

obligation dealt with the recognitions of your jurisdiction.

Those are dependent on circumstances of the

times. We may have recognized the Grand Lodge of

Cuba when you were made a Mason, but you are not

now allowed to communicate about the secrets of

Masonry with its members. We may have regarded the

Grand Lodge of Senegal as clandestine when you

became a Mason, but you may now visit their lodges

since our 1998 recognition of them.

Should we recognize the Prince Hall Grand Lodge of North Carolina, they would no longer be clandestine — they would be regular.

8. *Is our formation any more or less regular than Prince Hall Masonry?*

No. The Grand Lodge of North Carolina declared itself in 1787 from lodges already operating in North Carolina. Following the war with England, these lodges operated without a central body. The Prince Hall Grand Lodge of North Carolina was chartered by the Prince Hall Grand Lodge of New York in 1870.

9. *Do Prince Hall Masons memorize a catechism?*

The Prince Hall Grand Secretary of NC reports that they require memory work and return proficiency. Their candidates must learn the first and second degree before advancing. They do not permit more than one degree in a day, nor all three degrees in less than 30 days.

10. What are their fees and dues?

Their fees for the degrees average about $65, with

lodge dues ranging from $25 to $100.

11. Are our Grand Lodge Officers pressing for Prince Hall recognition?

The GL Officers did not initiate the proposed change.

One local lodge submitted the resolution, and was

subsequently joined by the two other lodges. Once submitted,

it must be brought before the GL of NC at our next

Annual Communication. Considering the importance,

passion, and diversity of opinions regarding this subject,

a task force was appointed to collect information,

share information, and make recommendations for and

to the Masons of the state. Grand Master Thomas W.

Gregory has announced his support of the recognition of

the Prince Hall Grand Lodge of North Carolina.

12. What if we extend recognition and they do not

reciprocate?

Nothing. Nothing can happen until an agreement between the Grand Lodges is reached.

13. If the delegates vote to approve recognition, does that mean Prince Hall Masons could visit my lodge?

While no compact has been negotiated, if full recognition were granted, Prince Hall members would qualify to visit a lodge of the Grand Lodge of North Carolina.

14. Could a Prince Hall Mason affiliate with my lodge if we pass this?

If full recognition is made, a Prince Hall member would be able join a Grand Lodge of North Carolina lodge, provided he went through the normal affiliation process and was elected, just like a Mason from the Grand Lodge of Vermont or other recognized grand lodge.

15. Isn't recognition really just a first step toward merger?

No. Each group has its own lodges, officers, and

history. Neither Grand Lodge wishes to give these up.

Each would remain autonomous.

16. Which Prince Hall Grand Lodge are we talking about?

There is only one Prince Hall Affiliate Grand Lodge

operating in North Carolina. The proposed recognition,

if approved as written, would only extend recognition to

the Prince Hall Affiliate Grand Lodge of North Carolina.

There are other groups operating in the state which

purport to be Masonic. Neither we nor the Prince Hall

Grand Lodge recognize these groups.

17. Some say that they have spoken with Prince Hall

acquaintances and they don't like the idea either. Why?

Individuals from both Grand Lodges have their own

opinions. No single individual necessarily represents

a majority.

18. I've heard Prince Hall Grand Lodge has no desire to

swap recognition, is that true?

No. Many of their members have expressed interest in Fraternal relations with our Grand Lodge, including their Grand Master Nathaniel Johnson.

19. Is Prince Hall Masonry in North Carolina currently recognized by the Grand Lodge of England?

No. In 1996 the United Grand Lodge of England recognized the grand lodge from which North Carolina Prince Hall Masonry descended as being regular. All other United States descendants recognized by the "regular" lodge with which they share jurisdiction have been recognized soon after requesting it of UGLE. Fifteen have been recognized as of this writing.

20. What requirements do Prince Hall lodges have for admission?

A man must believe in a supreme being, be of lawful age, free born, of good moral standing, well respected in the community, and gainfully employed.

21. Do they accept members with criminal records?

The Prince Hall Code states that no one who has

been convicted of a felony may be initiated or continue

membership.

22. Are their modes of recognition the same as ours?

Such modes of recognition are considered Masonic

secrets and not subject to discussion by either Grand

Lodge or its members. None of the other several dozen

jurisdictional recognitions has reported any problem in

this respect.

23. Are their rituals and obligations the same as ours?

Their ritual, as ours, is derived largely from the work

of Thomas Smith Webb. In the late 1700s and early

1800s Webb popularized much of the work currently

done in American lodges. His work is related to that of

William Preston, a predecessor who spread a version of

the work popular in British lodges today.

24. What about exclusive territorial jurisdiction?

Exclusive territorial jurisdiction is not universally accepted even by our own Grand Lodge. We recognize several grand lodges which share the same geographic territory. For instance, we have fraternal relations with several grand lodges in Brazil which share territory, some with lodges in the same city. They include Grande Loja Maconica Do Estado de Sao Paulo and Grande Oriente Do Brasil among others. We recognize the Grand Lodge of Massachusetts which maintains lodges in Panama, Chile, and Japan where we recognize other grand lodges. The United Grand Lodge of England maintains lodges in India, as well as several African and South American nations which have grand lodges of their own which we recognize and with which we maintain fraternal relations.

In January 1999 Rick Parsons ceased to accept letters

to the editor concerning the Prince Hall issue. In an article addressing his decision, Rick wrote:

IN THE NEWS

North Carolina Mason January/February 1999

The great experiment is over.

Open debate on the race issue is now closed.

Fresh or especially intelligent opinions will continue to be considered.

The experiment began when opponents of Prince Hall recognition complained (without foundation) that their views were being suppressed by The North Carolina Mason. In fact, their views were not being submitted to The NC Mason. If we don't receive it, we can't print it. As usual, it's easier to complain than act. Opponents were urged to express themselves. While those campaigning the hardest against recognition have been careful to keep their names from being associated with their views in a more public venue than the tiled lodge, some of their admirers have offered their views in writing for publication. We have published virtually every opinion we have gotten against recognition. About 25% of those in favor have been omitted from print due to considerations of space and further accusations of being unfair.

We now receive condemnations for publishing too much on the issue. The majority of the complaining comes again from critics of recognition. Once more, they will get their way, but this time the editor is in agreement with them.

Chapter 5

1999

In March of 1999, it was announced that the annual meeting would move to Charlotte. Though the change was made necessary because the Raleigh Memorial Auditorium had committed the normal time of our meeting to a production of Phantom of the Opera, the anti-Prince Hall people took it as a ploy to move to the western part of the state where their would be less rural influence.

In April, the opening of the Grand Lodge coincided with the publishing of the interim report by the Prince Hall Task force which stated, in part:

IN THE NEWS

North Carolina Mason   March/April 1999

Although the review of the audio tapes is not complete, the following results were reported from straw votes at the informal lodge meetings:

Lodges for 25 (6.5%)

Lodges against 169 (43.9%)

Lodges taking no position 64 (16.6%)

Lodges not participating 127 (32.9%)

The booklet containing lodge responses to the Prince Hall Recognition Resolution was promised to each of the 384 lodges in NC by Dec. 1, 1998. In response to some 22 lodges requesting that the booklet not be made available to so many persons, the Grand Master decided that only the Task Force members and a few designated persons would be provided a copy. One copy of the booklet would be be available at the Grand Lodge office in Raleigh for review by any of our members.

Recommendations and further actions from the Task Force will be forthcoming, after appropriate meetings have been held by the Task Force.

As disappointing and hurtful as the Listening sessions were, they were still a good predictor of how the good... white... Christian Masons of North Carolina felt. At the Grand Lodge meeting that year the vote against recognizing Prince Hall was totally one sided.

At the same Grand Lodge meeting a young attorney from eastern North Carolina, Clark Joyner, was elected Grand Master. The man came to the position with an agenda and one of the main features of that agenda was to get Prince Hall Masonry recognized as the reality it was.

The Grand Master had no fear, or reluctance, to offend anyone. At his District Meetings he delivered a resounding message based on his legal background: Masons swore to look at the interior of a man and not his exterior. Therefore, a Mason, a good Mason, couldn't be a racist... regardless of his reasoning. This attitude left many white Masons squirming. Grand Master Joyner simply wasn't going to hear a racist's attempt to explain why he would deny a Prince Hall Mason because of skin color.

When the new Grand Master agreed to a joint ceremony with Prince Hall Masons, tempers flared.

IN THE NEWS

North Carolina Mason   **September/October 1999**

Grand Lodge to Dedicate Charlotte's Freedom Bell

Charlotte — Masons will play yet another part in the history of this, North Carolina's largest city, this November. The Hezakiah Alexander house, built in 1774, has long been a center of life, tradition, democracy, and some say Freemasonry in Charlotte. On its grounds in October, the new Charlotte Museum of History will open. On November 5, our Grand Lodge will lay the cornerstone for Charlotte's American Freedom Bell. The 7.5-ton bronze bell will find its permanent home in a special pavilion at the museum, near the Alexander home. It has been touted as Charlotte's counterpart to the Liberty Bell in Philadelphia.

The ceremony is scheduled for 4:30 P. M., Friday, November 5. Officials have also invited the Prince Hall Grand Lodge to participate in the event. You're all invited to what promises to be one of the most important public Masonic events in years.

The Mecklenburg Declaration, signed in 1775, was a precursor to the Declaration of Independence. The bell is a monument to the spirit and philosophy of those 27 men who signed that document. Many of them were Masons. We hope to see you there as we complete the circle remembering our Brothers of 200 years ago and their spark that helped ignite our democracy.

Again, the letters, emails and discussion resumed.

Subject: Prince Hall issue

Sir:

It is with sadness and disgust that I feel the need to send this correspondence, but after having read the most recent issue of "The North Carolina Mason" I cannot in good conscience not respond. You mentioned things such as "un-Masonic conduct, learning to control and subdue our passions and prejudices, and our brethren comprising the entire human species."

On page 2, in the bottom left corner, is an article entitled "Prince Hall Recognitions Increasing." It is my feeling, sir, that one cannot truly talk of loving their families or their children until one is prepared to acknowledge that there are enemies who would destroy them, whether purposely or not, by destroying such things as their culture, and denying them access to their history, or rewriting it so that generations to follow, in effect, have no history.

Like it or not, the roots of a people start with their race, then proceed in a line down to their extended families. Considering that the black race is responsible for crime, destruction and receiving taxpayer funded government handouts far out of proportion to their representation in our society, I find it abominable that it is the goal of so many of you to have them involved in our Lodges.

How do you arrive at the notion that they are "our brethren"? I, sir, have no black "brethren". We have had to lower the standards in our education systems, and develop all sorts of programs, hand outs, legalized theft, etc. just to try to assimilate them into our society. The NAACP and all sorts of other black racist groups are allowed to permeate their lies and filth, with the help of their Jewish lawyers, with no cries of racism. We have become a bunch of gutless wonders, but deny it and say that it is "subduing our passions and prejudices." I think this whole thing is a money issue, with the money changers seeing all those dollars that they can't get ahold of. I'll be honest with you. It is late and I am not intentionally rambling, but I am on the verge of leaving Freemasonry forever if this issue continues like it is. Why don't you just come right out and say that you want blacks in the lodges? You're not fooling anyone with platitudes about "friendship and brotherly love" towards those who are causing us immeasurable harm. I can imagine a country much stronger with much more good will and very little crime or other related problems if there weren't any blacks here. Is a man expected to abandon common sense and true love to his family and friends when he becomes a Mason? Burying your head in the sand while citing parts of the oath and applying them to blacks will not change the truth!! And I suspect that you can fill your lodges with your "black brethren", but at a price — you will see very many men leave those lodges, men that you are counting on just to sit back and accept it!!!!

Our ancestors would turn over in their graves at the travesty that you are perpetrating!!

Prudence demands that I remain: Anonymous

The email above and the Grand Master's response both appeared in the September/ October 1999 issue of the *NC Mason*. Some of the comments of the email writer, who was anonymous, obviously aroused the ire of the Grand Master and those of us who felt above such hatred. The Grand Master's response quoted many items of Masonic structure that slammed directly at the writer and his racism. Of course, we were learning at this point that some of our "brothers" hated Blacks because that's the way they were raised, or they resented progress Blacks had made in this country, or they felt they were being discriminated against for being White, or... they just hated Blacks. But, regardless of their reason, NONE of them considered themselves racist.

A half-page of pictures and articles about the joint dedication of Charlotte's Freedom Bell in the *NC Mason* brought the racists out of the woodwork. The first sight of black and white faces together in a Masonic program let some know that what was coming was real, and it wasn't that far away.

At my lodge's monthly supper, Tallon Trask motioned for me to join him in the lobby. "Logan, this shit is real isn't it?" he asked almost whispering.

"Which shit is that Tallon?" I knew exactly what he was talking about, but by now it was a game.

"That Nigger thing. They gonna' force them down our

throats in spite of Hell, ain't they?" It was refreshing that he didn't shout his question so that everyone else could hear him. I had to wonder why? And wonder had someone else talked to him?

"Tallon, I don't know who you think 'they' are. I hope I'm part of that 'they' you're talking about."

"I'm talking about that Grand Lodge crowd," he said in a slur.

"Tallon, I'm a part of that Grand Lodge crowd, as you call them, and very proud of it."

"Okay, then I'll ask you, why are you people trying to cram those damn Niggers down our throats?"

I paused for a moment. I wanted to be at least Masonic about my answer.

"Tallon, you remember in our First Degree lecture when the man said that "Masonry regarded the internal and not the external of a man? You remember that?"

"Yea, but know as well as I do that they weren't talking about no Niggers."

"Well, who the hell do you think they were talking about, Tallon? They were talking about everyone. Don't you remember the word 'mankind'? That's everyone... Niggers, as you call them too."

He was quiet. Had I hit a nerve?

"Nobody's trying to shove anything down anybody's throat. All anyone is asking you to do is do what you've already promised... no, sworn to do. That's all."

Tallon didn't say a thing. It was almost scary. I wasn't stupid, a comment or two doesn't change a racists' mind. Yet, he was being quiet. Why?

"This stuff is serious, ain't it?" he asked in the same whispered manner..

"Serious as a heart attack."

Again, Tallon was quiet. Good or bad , I didn't know, but the guy was thinking.

"Logan, I love Masonry as much as anybody. Masonry's a good thing. It's a part of my life. But, it's changing. It's changing big time. And I don't know how to handle it."

For the first time, I almost felt sorry for him... almost.

"No, Tallon, Masonry isn't changing. It's been the same for three hundred years. It's just that people like you tried to make it the way you wanted to see it. Not the way it really was."

I had gone to the Grand Lodge building in Raleigh for the year's first meeting of the Masonic Education committee and while I was there, I went into the editor of the *NC Mason*'s office and we sat for a chat. I knew he had been beaten to death because of his support for Prince Hall recognition. We had been friends for a long time and I figured about now he needed a friend.

"Boy," I said, "you've caught hell haven't you?"

"Yea, but I knew it was going to be that way from the beginning. I guess anything worthwhile is rough... and I know this is worthwhile. Maybe I'm a fool, but that's the way I feel."

"I agree, but sometime don't you just want to say screw it and move on to something else?"

"Maybe, but then I remember how much I love this fraternity and what it stands for. When I think of that I figure what the hell? Am I going to let a few Rednecks take it away? Then... it becomes something worth fighting for."

"Yea," I said. "I see what you mean. I knew it was going to be bad, but I didn't know it was going to be this bad."

"There," he said, "I've got an advantage. I'm from the coast. Down there we've got people still fighting the Civil War... at least in their heads. They haven't accepted that the South lost."

"I'll agree," I said. "You got some doozies down there."

"It was the way they were raised. To them anything that's not white is a Nigger and can't be trusted. In a way I can't blame them. Some of them have been crapped on all their lives. They're poor, half-uneducated and ... whatever. They've got to blame somebody. They can't blame Mama. They won't blame Papa and one thing is damn sure... they won't blame themselves. Which, by all rights is where the blame should fall. No, they got to blame somebody and for generations it's been the Blacks. Now, we're telling them we want the Blacks in our lodges. I can halfway see how they feel, but that doesn't make it right. That doesn't make it right at all."

The next morning I was talking with one of the guys on the Prince Hall task force and asked him what they had found about the ritual. Was the Prince Hall ritual anything remotely like ours?

"Can't tell you," he said.

"What do you mean you can't tell me? Is it some sort of secret?

"No," he said, "we haven't figured out how to tell. We don't know where to ask."

At that point, something seemed wrong. They had been working on the project over a year and didn't know this basic yet? "Do you want me to find out for you?" I asked in an almost angry tone. No, it wasn't almost. I was angry.

"You know we can't just ask the Prince Hall people about their ritual. They're not going to just hand it over to us. We wouldn't hand over ours."

I guess he was trying to play Mason with all the secrecy stuff, but somehow, it just came across as sounding petty.

That same morning, I put "Masonic Ritual" in my computer and got page after page of information. One web page was a book store in New York advertising the ritual for sale. I phoned the number.

"I need to get a copy of the Prince Hall ritual. What do I need to do?"

"We just call it the 'ritual'," said the man who sounded black and was probably a Prince Hall Mason. "All I need is an address and I can send it out today."

"Okay, I said, but I haven't paid you."

"I'm not worried about it," said the man. "We trust fellow Masons. I'll put a note in the package. Just send us a check."

I was floored. My Grand Lodge required payment in full before anything was sent out. They had learned their lesson the hard way from Masons who hadn't paid. Now, some little book store in New Your who didn't know me from Adam was sending me two copies of the ritual before they received a single dime simply because I was a Mason. This Prince Hall group may be a bit more Masonic than even I believed.

Within a couple of days I received a small package. Inside was two simple black books. As soon as I got them I opened one and poured through it. Every word, every lecture, every action, was almost exactly like ours. Every Grand Lodge has some variations, but the Prince Hall ritual was closer to being a duplicate of ours that the rituals I had seen from South Carolina and Virginia.

I spent the entire afternoon calling everyone I could think of. I was wanting to share the information about the Prince Hall ritual, I guess, more from happiness and excitement than for information. And, maybe a bit of joy to know for certain the Prince Hall ritual wasn't all that different than ours.

All through his year, the Grand Master Joyner had asked for change and also return. He wanted to change by becoming more visible to the community and less of the "secret organization" we were said to be. He wanted us to polish-up our act by returning to the days when Masons dressed for their meetings as they would for church. Little was said about becoming more visible, most members agreed with the concept. But, the idea of dressing-up for meetings struck a bare nerve.

Most North Carolina Masons are blue-collar workers and the idea of a coat and tie, or even just a tie, is entirely foreign to their lifestyle. Many of the lodges long ago abandoned a dress code. In some lodges the coat and tie was replaced by pants and a shirt and, in some lodges, just a tee-shirt became common. Any negative comment was quickly defended by the rationale of "that's what I wear to work and I come to lodge from work". For some of us, and definitely the Grand Master, such a dress code was unforgivable. The same group who took offense at the Grand Master's stand on supporting recognition of Prince Hall Masonry took offense to his stand on a dress code. And, the year 2000 Annual Communication was their opportunity to make their feelings known.

Dozens of the delegates to the meeting came wearing blue jeans and tee shirts. Although the designs on the tee shirts were varied, many of the tee shirts were emblazoned with Confederate flags. There was no question as to the wearer's intent.

With the exception of those dressed like they were attending a Klan picnic, the communication itself was relatively civil. As the event proceeded, there were a few more boos and negative comments than usual about anything that could be construed as supporting the Recognition issue, but most of the ones against recognition were somewhat restrained. When the vote to share jurisdiction came, it was a sound two to one defeat. Cheers greeted the announcement.

I had spoken to Rick Parson, but this was his busy time so I knew I wouldn't see much of him. But, when the vote was announced I saw him in the distance absolutely glowing. I was confused.

Later, he walked by where I was sitting and I cornered him.

"Why were you grinning like a Cheshire cat when they announced the vote? Don't you know... we lost again?"

"No, we didn't," he said.

"Am I missing something?" I asked. "It sounded like..."

"Dude, we won. Think about it. Last year's vote was four to one against. This year, it was two to one against. All that crap we've been doing is paying off. We doubled last year."

Rick was right. In one year, we had doubled what we had done before.

Though the vote on Prince Hall held center stage at the meeting, other decisions would change the events of the next few years. Our present Grand Master was a firebrand. He was verbal about his support for Prince Hall recognition and equally verbal about his desire to make other changes in the fraternity. But, the man who replaced him was the exact opposite.

Our next Grand Master was the personification of the word 'gentle'. If he ever made a statement in support of Prince Hall recognition or a statement critical of anything I can't remember it. Every word he spoke and every paragraph he wrote seemed to be designed NOT to offend anyone. Yet, his time would be short.

At the same communication, it was decided to change the annual meeting from April to September. This meant that

Grand Master Eldridge's term would be short. Though Eldridge was a likeable man, those of us pushing for Prince Hall recognition knew it would not come under his watch. To so many, the thought of granting any form of equality to a group of Blacks was offensive. And, Grand Master Eldridge made it a point not to offend anyone.

But, we didn't worry. In the wings, the next Grand Master, would be Albert Mimms, another attorney, but this time from the other end of the state. Like the former Grand Master, he knew no fear, he considered recognition the only Masonic way and he would go headlong against anything he considered non-Masonic.

Those six months passed quickly and though we knew Eldridge was a good man and a wonderful Mason, those of us crying for support of the Prince Hall issue needed what was to come... Albert Mimms. We had no doubt that he was going to do things that had never been done and force things that had never been forced. He was verbal about Prince Hall recognition not only being the right thing to do, but being the only thing to do. Yet, those opposed to Prince Hall were still there and still strong We didn't know how strong until September.

The business for the year had actually been concluded at the April meeting. Our first September meeting was to be little more than a handful of formalities, elect Mimms Grand Master and go home. Great, but it didn't work that way. When it came time for the election everything seemed normal until the ballots for Grand Master were counted. Mimms fell twenty-two votes short of what was needed for election. In a subsequent vote he faired no better. Speeches and hand wringing of various degrees followed, but in the end... Mimms lost. The hero of our movement into the twentieth century was defeated.

I actually dreaded going to my next lodge supper because I didn't know how Mimms' defeat would be viewed by those in the lodge. I was sure Tallon Trask would be revived, but I didn't know how many others the defeat would drag out of the woodwork. But, actually I was surprised. The event was mentioned, but it was more in passing than the blast I had expected. The most surprising was Tallon Trask. He said nothing. He greeted me when I sat down, but other than that, he was totally quiet.

We hated to see our flag-bearer defeated, but the man who was ultimately elected was far from a slouch to our cause. Unlike Mimms, who would advertise his feelings to anyone who would listen, Bill Breen had been rather quiet. In a surprise moment in his inaugural address he asked the question, "When you say Masonry, do you mean Masonic lodges that are fortresses for bigots and braggarts?" and followed up with his commitment to take us into the twenty-first century. He also made this clear, very clear, in his first column in the *NC Mason.*

I Called Rick at the Grand Lodge after I got my issue of the paper. "We're going to be okay, aren't we?" I asked.

"Yep, Breen fooled them all. They figured since he was from the coast he probably had a white sheet and hood in his closet. They couldn't have been any wronger. He's smart. He'll do the right thing"

"Wronger," I chuckled. "Is wronger a word?"

"It is for this. This guy is intelligent and sharp. He's not the loser they want."

"Where does that put us?" I asked.

"I say full steam ahead. You get that committee of yours geared up and throw another set of Prince Hall lessons out this summer and in the paper. You can have as much space in the *Mason* as you need."

"Is it safe to assume there's going to be some more black faces in the paper?"

"You said that. I didn't."

I knew Rick well enough to know that he was grinning when he said it.

"By the way," he said. "Breen is creating a commission on fraternal relations."

"Great, what's that?" I asked.

"He has found some of the highest power Masons in the state to be on his commission and study this thing."

"High power," I asked. "Who are they?"

"Just wait until it comes out. You're not going to believe it."

"I was curious who would be on the commission, but I also knew there were lots of high-power Masons from which to choose.

I wouldn't have to wait long. The March/April issue had the announcement as the headline article.

IN THE NEWS

North Carolina Mason   **March/April 2001**

Commission on Fraternal Relations Begins Work

Greensboro — North Carolina

Freemasonry's most difficult problem now has an all-star team pursuing answers.

Grand Master Breen's Commission on Fraternal Relations, the highest powered group gathered by the Grand Lodge in many years, has been charged to redefine our Grand Lodge's relationship with the North Carolina Prince Hall Grand Lodge. On the commission is a past Governor, a past chief of staff in the US Congress, a past NC Attorney General and a current Federal Court Judge. The Commission is being chaired by a past NC Supreme

Court Chief Justice.

Since talk began about recognizing the Prince Hall Grand Lodge of North Carolina, a top criticism of the movement has been that the details of the proposed relationship were not clear. Grand Master Breen and North Carolina Prince Hall Grand Master Marvin Willis decided that a joint committee could best develop those details. Willis is likewise appointing a four man commission to work with Brantley's appointed group. The AF & AM group held its first meeting in Greensboro March 23. They were charged by Grand Master Breen to "promote harmonious relations" and present an acceptable proposal for "reciprocal recognition" between the two organizations.

The first joint meeting has yet to be set. At press time, the names of the Prince Hall appointments were not available.

The day the paper came out was the same day as our lodge meeting. I was running late and went straight from work to the lodge. When I walked in the door I was greeted by Adam Fields who is usually a rather mild type. "Logan, Trask tells me you're a part of this crap, and I can't believe it."

"What are you talking about, Adam?" I asked totally taken off guard.

"That task force that Nigger loving Grand Master of yours put together."

"I've heard something about it, but obviously you know more than I do," I said.

"It was in that claprag we got it today. You ain't seen it?"

"No, I came straight from...."

"Hell," he reached across the table and grabbed a copy of the paper. "They got governors and senators and supreme court judges and everything but God on the thing. There ain't a real Mason on the thing. There ain't no truck drivers or mechanics. None of them people are real Masons. I can't believe it. Read it!"

Part of what Fields said was true. The Grand Master had put Past Governor Saunders, a past chief of staff in the US Congress, a past attorney general and a couple of supreme court justices on the commission. Rick had been right. This was a high-power group.

"Whatcha' think of it? You see what they're doing? They're real about this stuff. They're gonna' throw the doors wide open for them Niggers."

Field's naivety floored me. Where had he been for the past two years? "Adam, why are you so surprised. This thing has been going on for two years. Where were you? This isn't anything new."

"No, maybe not, but I just thought it was a handful of pinky-assed liberals making some noise. But these people is dead serious."

"I've been trying to tell you. It's coming. It's right. And, it's coming," I said.

I was still in wonder at Tallon Trask. He had said nothing.

Up until that point, all the conversation about Prince Hall recognition had been dinner-time chatter. Yes, some of it had been serious, but it was still dinner-time chatter. But, that night, Fields continued his rage into the meeting itself. Since it was a form of politics, such conversations are a total no-no and forbidden in a Masonic lodge.

Fields stood and was acknowledged by the Master. "I don't know who saw it, but there was an article in the *NC Mason* today about the Prince Halls. Brothers, this thing is getting way out of hand. When they start appointing governors, and I don't know what all, to these committees, it ain't just conversation. And, I want to know what we can do about it."

The Master was quiet for a time then spoke. "Brother Fields, I hesitate to discuss this in the lodge because, no matter how you cut it, it's politics. And, we don't discuss politics or religion in the lodge. But, since this is an emotional issue. Some of you who haven't said a word have talked to me about it. I believe we should discuss it... a little."

The Master looked at me. "Brother Logan, I believe you are on the Grand Lodge Education Committee. How would you answer Brother Fields' question? What can we do about it?"

"Master," I replied, "the Grand Lodge has sponsored listening sessions and the Education Committee had programs on this throughout the state last year. There's been something in the paper every time it came out. And now, it appears nobody knew anything about it."

The Master nodded and motioned for me to continue.

"First thing, no one has proposed that we merge with Prince Hall. That's never been mentioned. Second, we're not throwing the doors open for anyone. All that's asked is that we recognize them as Masons... real Masons. That's all."

Someone blurted, "But they're not real Masons. Coloreds can't be real Masons. I been in Masonry for over thirty years and I heard that since the beginning."

"Well, they can," I said. "Every year, the Grand Lodge recognizes some grand lodge in Africa, in the Bahamas, somewhere that's predominately Black. We recognize Blacks all the time. The only difference with Prince Hall is they don't live ten thousand miles away."

There was total silence in the lodge. I waited a minute then spoke. "Gentlemen, Brothers, there's nothing drastic about recognizing Prince Hall. In their community these men are the best of the best. If a man has gone to prison and served his time, we'll take him as a member. They won't. There's a lot of other things we'll do, that they won't. And, to answer Brother Fields' question... what can you do about it? Truthfully, nothing. And, truthfully, you shouldn't want to. The train has left the station and it's headed for the twenty-first century. What everyone in this lodge needs to do is find out what it means... the truth. My suggestion is you go to one of the Masonic Education seminars this summer. Write down your questions... bring them. But guys, leave the crap about one race being inferior to another at home. That just doesn't work any more."

I could feel a few hateful stares when I sat down, but somehow what I had said was good. I saw Tallon Trask pass a glance at me, but his face didn't betray how he was feeling.

Later, when I got home, I called Rick. "I stepped square into it tonight, Bro."

He laughed. He knew why. "There's an old thing about the power of things in print. That's why I didn't tell you. I wanted you to get the same impact."

"Well... it worked."

I told him about the events at the lodge.

"I'm not surprised," he said. "Some of these people think it's all a big joke. It isn't real. Oh hell... the loudmouths are yelling, but that's what they do. That's not the ones we need to worry about. We need to worry about the quiet ones. They've got a vote too."

"Guess I know what the summer sessions need to be about."

"Yea, I guess you do, but I believe they'll be a bit better attended than in the past. I believe they'll be a whole lot better attended," Rick said with absolute certainty.

Then he asked a question, "You are aware, aren't you, that the loudmouths we're hearing aren't the head of the monster? There's a lot smarter creatures pulling the strings."

"Somehow, I knew that," I answered. "The ones I'm seeing on the Internet and writing articles haven't got enough sense to keep from crapping on themselves."

"That's right. They're just the mouths. There's a couple of Past Grand Masters actually pulling their strings. The ones you hear are just puppets," he said.

"Yea, I thought that," I said.

"And while I've got you," I said. "There's one question that still keeps popping up. I know Sands said we're doing it because it's the right thing to do, and Green put the religious twist in it by saying a good Christian would never condemn a man because of his race and Grand Master Joyner said the same thing every time somebody gave him the chance, but one question continues to keep coming up. Has Prince Hall asked to be recognized?"

Parsons' answer was at first simple, "No," then he explained. "Evidently, you are like the majority of our guys. You haven't seen exactly how classy... how Masonic... these Prince Hall people are. They are taking the attitude that this entire thing is our fight, not theirs and they're not going to get involved in our fight. Unsaid, and very unsaid, is as far as they're concerned, the fact that we would even have people who are racist, or bigoted or whatever you want to call it, is in itself unmasonic and our problem."

"But don't they have people who don't want to have anything to do with 'Whitey'?" I asked.

"I'm sure they do," he said, "but they don't go shouting

it to anyone who'll listen. As far as they're concerned, the rule is simple... it is the interior and you know the rest."

"Yea, I know," I said.

"No, these guys aren't going to get involved in washing our laundry. We created the mess and it'll be ours to undo. I just hope that when our laundry is washed and clean, we don't find out it's Klan robes."

"Yea, I do too," I said. "I do too."

Parsons knew what was going on, there was no doubt about that, but he was right there in the center of the thing. Things that were complementary were called to the Grand Lodge office, and things that were critical were definitely called there too. While I had him, I wanted as many answers as I could get.

"You know the image is 'Grand Lodge against everybody else and the Grand Lodge is shoving this down our throats'," I said.

"Sure, I do," Parsons responded. "But it's because we're the obvious. You think for one minute this Prince Hall thing could have continued even this long if there weren't people in the lodges, not the Grand Lodge, but in the normal rank and file lodges, who didn't feel it was right, and didn't want it? They like to say the Grand Lodge is shoving it down our throats, but if no one wanted it, when Sands began this whole thing, that would have been the end of it. Yet, it wasn't and that's because there's enough out there who think it is right. But hell, we can't expect them to take state-wide stands on these things. That's our job."

Rick was right about the attendance at the Summer Seminars. The Masonic Education Committee conducted twelve meetings at various places across the state. In some meetings extra chairs had to be brought in. Each of the ones conducting the meetings were selected because of their ability to control a situation. Many were past Grand Masters who had an excellent ability to conduct meetings. There wasn't a concern that the meetings would get out of hand as many of the Listening Sessions had done, but that one or two loudmouths would try to monopolize the meeting undermining the educational value.

In all, the meetings went well because the entire session was directed at educating the members about Prince Hall Masonry... what it was and what it wasn't. The meetings also followed a pattern we had hoped for. Without exception, some bigot would lead off with a purely racial comment and the one leading the meeting would let them know the purpose of the meeting was to discuss the Prince Hall organization, not race. This pulled the rug from such questions for the balance of the meeting.

After each group of meetings, the presenters compared notes over the telephone. We knew we had something good when it appeared every session was followed by a comment like, "I didn't realize that." And, while this was gratifying, it wasn't entirely understood. Nothing new was brought up at these sessions. The information provided came straight from previous items that had been published in the *NC Mason* or sent out to the lodges. Every item had been mentioned before. It made no sense.

I called Rick and told him.

"Do you think some of the ones who were so busy running off at the mouth may just be listening?" he asked.

It was an interesting question.

The first part of 2002 continued with the same bickering and name calling on the Internet that the previous years had seen. But, somehow, there was an unexplained mellowness in the exchanges. Nothing new had been said in several years. The same criticisms and defenses that had been exchanged since the beginning continued to be bounced around and it was apparent both sides were becoming bored.

Nothing happened of any substance until the amendments that would be considered at the 2002 Grand Lodge session were announced. The amendment to require a two-thirds majority to pass any recognition of another Grand Lodge and the amendment to ban any amendment that had been voted on in the past five years came to life. The ones supporting recognition had played all their cards. The education programs and meetings designed to inform had been presented in one form or another for the past three years. Granted, they had some effect, but not enough. There was little more those in favor of recognition could do.

On the other side, those against recognition had a totally new tool. Seeing that the passage of recognition of Prince Hall Masonry was apparently little more than months away, yet knowing they still possessed a simple majority, the two-thirds requirement was ideal. With the amendment on the table and its potential to delay recognition for years, the anti crowd mustered their forces.

Little was said in my lodge about the Prince Hall issue and for several months it remained virtually a non-issue, until the list of proposed amendments appeared in the *NC Mason*.

On an August evening Brother Fields brought up the issue in his normal manner. "Logan, I see they're gonna' vote on requiring a two-thirds majority to recognize yer' people."

"Yea, looks like they're gonna' vote on something like that."

"You know it'll pass... don't you?" he asked.

"No, I don't know. Maybe it will. Maybe it won't. We'll see."

"Crap, Logan, you know it's gonna' pass and so is that five year thing."

"Five year thing?" I asked. I knew what he was talking

about, but I would have rotted before I would have admitted it.

"Yea, if somethin's turned down you can't vote on it for five more years. That's the way it should be anyhow. My god, how many times you gotta' vote on the same thing?"

"Adam, I don't know how it's going to turn out, but I do know that as long as a lodge wants to present something for a vote they have to have a chance. That's the rules."

I almost thought I saw Tallon Trask smile, but I'm not certain.

"I don't know about rules, but I'm gonna' be up there and I'm gonna' vote for the right thing," said Fields.

Henry Blake spoke up. I guess he was about tired of Field's mouth. "Fields, how you going to vote? You're not a lodge officer. You haven't even done what's required to become a lodge officer."

"How you figure that? Maybe I'm not a lodge officer, but I'm sure as hell a member of the Grand Lodge."

"Yea, you are a member, but you're not a voting member. Only the Master and Wardens can vote."

I couldn't help it. To see this know-it-all squirm was... well, I chuckled.

"What the hell you laughing at Logan? If I ain't got no vote, you ain't got no vote."

"I have a vote, Adam."

"How you got a vote? You ain't no lodge officer."

"No," I replied, "I'm not a lodge officer, but I am on a Grand Lodge committee. Committee members get a vote."

"Well, ain't that some shit?" Fields said as he walked off.

The next month, when the votes were counted it appeared the anti-recognition group had orchestrated their game well. The amendment to require a two-thirds majority passed with no problem, but the amendment to prevent a revote on a defeated issue was ruled out of order. It was decided that no rule should ever be passed that would bind future delegates removing their opportunity to govern the organization. Again, the amendment to share jurisdiction, recognize Prince Hall Masonry, was defeated. But, by less of a margin.

Even though Masonry in North Carolina appeared still locked in the past, other parts of the nation appeared more realistic. That year, Missouri, another former slave state, recognized Prince Hall as did New Jersey. And, the first black Mason was voted in as a member in a regular Winston Salem lodge. The house of cards wasn't gone, but it was definitely crumbling.

Chapter 6

2003

In January of 2003 the report of the Commission on
the Recognition of Prince Hall Masonry in North Carolina
was issued. The rather lengthy report covered every
conceivable item that had been used to refuse recognition.
The bottom line was that Black Masonry was, indeed,
regular and that in all good conscience, there was no reason
to not immediately approve recognition. The report ended

IN THE NEWS

North Carolina Mason   **January/ February 2003**

"To fail to pass this resolution will be seen by Masons

and non-Masons in North Carolina, other states, and the world to be nothing more than discrimination against Brother Masons on the basis of race. It will damage the Grand Lodge and Freemasonry in the eyes of most people and will hinder the future growth and prosperity of our fraternity. Brother Martin eloquently reminded the Grand Lodge in 2001 that:

This issue has been before this Grand Lodge since 1947. With an improvement in race relations and understanding, there has been a growing readiness in some Southern States, including Virginia and North Carolina, to begin a more enlightened consideration of the universality of Freemasonry. As a large majority of our sister grand lodges in America have affirmed the legitimacy of Prince Hall Freemasonry, there can be no pretense of any Masonic principle that would deny granting the same recognition to Prince Hall Masons as we have granted to other grand jurisdictions. Even more compelling is the need to settle this issue in a way that will advance the future of Freemasonry. America today is a land of equality of opportunity. It is a bastion for religious and philosophical tolerance. Few of our young men hold to views on racial separation such as were more common only decades ago. There is still a propensity for "birds of a feather to flock together," but there is very little acceptance today of rules or organizations that would compel segregation based on race. That is why today there are no statutory social distinctions in Masonry. The Grand Lodge should heed these words both of encouragement and warning. The Commission strongly believes that extending mutual fraternal recognition to Prince Hall Grand Lodge is necessary to ensure that Freemasonry in North Carolina will prosper in the future as it has in the past. To defeat such a proposal will be a step backward for our brotherhood and will be the source of damaging, negative repercussions for years to come.

About the time the report was issued, Rick Parsons offered to answer questions about Prince Hall Masonry in his "From The Editor's Desk" column in the *NC Mason.*

"Is that a wise thing to do?" I asked.

"Why? Haven't we been doing it all along?" responded Rick.

"As things came up, you did an article or something but you haven't openly asked for questions," I said.

"True, but I'm not worried about it," said Rick. "Have you heard one new statement or one new question in the past five years? It's always the same rehash. I guess they figure if they ask enough times, the answer will change. I'm just giving them the chance to rehash it again."

"Still sounds risky to me. Aren't you opening the door to some of the loudmouths?" I asked.

"Not really. I said I would answer questions. I will answer questions... I didn't say a thing about giving some loudmouth page or two to vent the some bigoted crap."

"Some of them are very creative," I responded still concerned..

"Taking their questions and answering them can't hurt a thing. Information is the only way we'll win. Right?

"Yea."

"What happens at those seminars of yours? Some loudmouth gets up and asks some question about Prince Hall designed to hurt and you answer the question. What happens?"

"Usually nothing. He grunts and sits down," I answered.

"Right. Except in the Masonic Education seminars they may want to argue or at least bitch a little, but the answer is still out there. They can't change that. Even if the guy is too stupid to understand the answer, even if he doesn't like it, it's out there. Everyone in that room has heard it. In this case, putting it in the *NC Mason*, the answer is out there to fifty thousand other people and I don't have to hear the bitching. It'll work."

"I hope so."

"I know so," said Rick. "Besides, is there a question... one question, they could ask that you'd rather avoid? Is there a question they could ask that we should be ashamed to answer? No. All these people are afraid of is that some black face may turn up in his lodge. That's all."

Rick was right, and the questions did come in, but just as he had predicted, they were the same old questions that had been answered over and over again.

In April, the two Commissions, the Commission from our Grand Lodge created by Grand Master Breen two years earlier, and the Commission from the Most Worshipful

Prince Hall Grand Lodge of North Carolina, sat down together to begin work. Rick went out of his way to report this in the *Mason.*

"Do you people pay one bit of attention to what we're saying?" asked Brother Fields at my next lodge meeting.

"As usual, Fields, I don't know what you are talking about."

"They keep turning down those Prince Halls at Grand Lodge, but damn, that don't matter. You people start having meetings on how we gonna' get together with 'em. Don't what we say mean a damn thing?"

"You just can't see the forest for the trees can you?" I asked. "All those votes you seem to be so proud of are just stalling the inevitable. It's going to pass. It may even pass this year, but if it doesn't, it will sometime."

"You people just can't leave well enough alone."

"Evidently, we can't," I said.

In July, the resolution of the Prince Hall Commission was published.

IN THE NEWS

North Carolina Mason **July/August 2003**

RESOLUTION OF MUTUAL RECOGNITION OF THE MOST WORSHIPFUL PRINCE HALL GRAND LODGE OF FREE AND ACCEPTED MASONS OF NORTH CAROLINA AND ITS JURISDICTIONS, INC. BY THE MOST WORSHIPFUL GRAND LODGE OF ANCIENT, FREE AND ACCEPTED MASONS OF NORTH CAROLINA

> **WHEREAS**, The Most Worshipful Grand Lodge of Ancient, Free and Accepted Masons of North Carolina (hereinafter "The Grand Lodge") desires to insure a continuing harmonious relationship between it and The Most Worshipful Prince Hall Grand Lodge of Free and Accepted Masons of North Carolina and its Jurisdictions, Inc. (hereinafter "The Prince Hall Grand Lodge"); to provide for the successful coexistence of both Grand Lodges and to promote Masonry in general among all peoples;
>
> **AND WHEREAS,** The Grand Lodge, for all the

reasons set out in Brother James G. Martin's Statement to The Grand Lodge dated September 29, 2001, a copy of which is attached hereto and incorporated by reference, believes that it is altogether right and proper and in the best interests of Masonry everywhere and particularly in North Carolina that these two Grand Lodges exercising Masonic jurisdiction in this state mutually recognize each other while each retains its own autonomy and jurisdiction hereafter as heretofore; AND WHEREAS, The Grand Lodge is satisfied that The Prince Hall Grand Lodge meets all Masonic requirements for recognition;

AND WHEREAS, The Grand Lodge desires to remain autonomous within its jurisdiction and to operate hereafter as heretofore with its own Grand Master and other Grand Lodge officers, Constitution, By-Laws, Ritual, Rules and Regulations, and to retain its absolute and supreme sovereignty over its own Subordinate Lodges and Membership;

AND WHEREAS, The Grand Lodge is advised that The Prince Hall Grand Lodge entertains the same desires and possesses the same satisfaction with regard to recognition by it of The Grand Lodge and desires that both Grand Lodges mutually recognize each other as duly constituted Masonic Grand Lodges;

AND WHEREAS, The Grand Lodge is advised that The Prince Hall Grand Lodge at its Annual Communication in 2003 will likely consider a resolution

extending fraternal recognition to The Grand Lodge in the same manner and on the same terms as the present resolution,

NOW, THEREFORE, BE IT RESOLVED BY THE MOST WORSHIPFUL GRAND LODGE OF ANCIENT, FREE AND ACCEPTED MASONS OF NORTH CAROLINA THAT:

1. It hereby extends fraternal recognition to The Prince Hall Grand Lodge of Free and Accepted Masons of North Carolina and Its Jurisdictions, Inc., (hereinafter "The Prince Hall Grand Lodge") as a duly constituted Masonic Grand Lodge;

2. It will remain autonomous within its jurisdiction and will operate hereafter as

heretofore with its own Grand Master and other Grand Lodge Officers, Constitution, By-Laws, Ritual, Rules and Regulations and will retain its absolute and supreme sovereignty over its own Subordinate Lodges and Membership;

3. This resolution shall become effective at such time as The Prince Hall Grand Lodge adopts a resolution extending fraternal recognition to The Grand Lodge in the same manner and on the same terms as the present resolution.

Three months later, the Grand Lodge met again and the vote on Prince Hall recognition once more failed, but by less than forty votes, still far beyond the now required two-thirds.

At he same meeting, a motion was introduced to do away with the two-third requirement and return to a simple majority. But, it would be another year before that vote could be taken.

Chapter 7

2004

In December of 2003, a man from the coast was installed as our new Grand Master. Many of the antis were certain he would go along with their way of thinking. Why? Simply because he was from the coast, historically, a hot bed for anti black feeling.

One week after our Grand Lodge session, in the exact same room, another meeting was held. This meeting, another Grand Lodge meeting, was held by the Most Worshipful Prince Hall Grand Lodge. Gone were the tee shirts, jeans and flip flops. The Prince Hall delegates were attired in tuxedos and business suits. One comment the Grand Master noted was the sound of applause from men wearing gloves was much different than the bare hands of the AF&AM delegates

It was the privilege of our Grand Master to address the group and unlike my Grand Lodge, which had rejected the proposal to recognize Prince Hall, the Prince Hall delegates voted to recognize my Grand Lodge unanimously.

The activities of the two Grand Lodges didn't go unnoticed. In December, an article appeared in the *News & Observer*, one of the two largest newspapers in the state giving a blow by blow account of the Masonic events of the previous few weeks. I first became aware of the article when I got a call from Axel Lyons, an older member of the lodge who usually kept a low profile.

"Have you seen the article in the *News & Observer*?" he asked. I had no idea what he was talking about.

"There's an article in the paper that paints us out as a bunch of Ku Kluxers. It's a horrible article. The whole world's gonna' see it. Go get the paper."

As soon as he hung up I looked up the article on the Internet. It was a good article... quite good, in fact. I called Rick.

"What do you know about the article?" I asked.

"Whew... damn phone's been ringing off the hook all morning. People are mad as hell. Want to know what we're going to do about it."

"Do about it?" I asked.

"Yea, like there's something we can do. Have you seen the article?" he asked.

"Yea, just read it on the Internet."

"It's a damn good article. The guy has all his facts and numbers. I think it makes us look better than we deserve."

"I didn't think it was all that bad, but I got a call this morning..."

"You got a call? Everybody in this office has been on the phone since we opened. Every light on this phone is lit. Some of these clowns want us to sue the paper."

"I just ask them to tell me which part is untrue."

"What do they say?"

"They don't say anything. Most of 'em just cuss and hang up."

"You been cussed at before."

"Oh yea."

Over the next few weeks, other papers throughout the

state picked up the article or ran their own articles about the racial situation. One columnist, a Mason, ran an article publicly resigning his membership and urging other Masons to do the same. One article cited men who had resigned their jobs after their employers questioned their membership in a "racist" organization.

Chapter 8

True Fraternity

At this point, as it is said, the die was cast. The old battles of "they're not real Masons" and "I swore not to sit in a lodge with one" had lost its punch. For the first time, even those who had made such statements heard themselves and became aware of how unimportant they sounded. Many who had lived by the notion of "I was told..." had to realize that the one doing the telling, may just be wrong.

Somehow, the anger, the urgency, on both sides of the issue gradually subsided. The violent verbal attacks seemed to... quite simply... go away.

I believe the best memory I have of that three year limbo was a conversation I had with Rick Parsons at the Grand Lodge building.

"You haven't said much in the *North Carolina Mason.* Why?" I asked.

"No point," he answered. "It's done."

"Are you saying you're giving up?" I asked surprised at the possibility.

"No, we won," he said with a somber air of certainty. "It's all falling into place. We did it."

I'm sure I looked confused.

"In the next few months somebody's going to introduce an amendment to return to a simple majority for recognition. The two-thirds thing was silly anyhow. It was just some loser's way of holding onto something that should have never existed in the first place for a few more days. Even they knew it wouldn't last. As soon as that change is made, well... the next step is recognition. It, my friend, is a done deal."

I think what struck me was the fact the Rick was right. For all intents and purposes, it was over.

Just as Rick predicted, the two-thirds amendment was introduced and one year later, the vote was taken Recognition passed 642 to 328.

For the first time in the almost three hundred years of Masonry in North Carolina members of the two Grand Lodges were brothers.

It's been too long in coming, but a new day

is finally dawning for Freemasonry in North

Carolina. We are finally moving into a time of

embracing our own teachings — taking those

teachings for their obvious meaning, rather than

straining interpretations to fit the society that

surrounded us.

We began to confront the truth and the problem

some years ago. As other Masonic jurisdictions

began to recognize Prince Hall Masonry,

we began the conversation here. Our talking led

to increasing self-examination. We found ourselves

lacking.

Freemasonry had stopped hearing its own

heartbeat of "friendship, morality, and brotherly

love." We had begun bending our rules to

the community that surrounded us, rather than

bringing our communities around to our ideals.

We were finally left with no choice but to face

our fraternity's struggle with racism.

It was impossible for a black man to become

a Mason in our Grand Lodge. It was even written

in our law for some 60 years. Removing *The Code's*

anti-black wording in the 1970s did not remove the

barrier.

Not to be denied the power and warmth and social

teachings of Freemasonry, black men developed

their own Masonic structure nearly 140 years ago and

Prince Hall Masonry thrived in North Carolina. Yet, we

could not bring ourselves to acknowledge that they

practiced the same brand of Masonry as we do.

"These two problems became the big secret in

Tar Heel Freemasonry. " They became the big lie,

a cancer on all our Craft's teachings. "The lie in

many ways came to permeate the organization.

It affected all that we did or tried to do.

We saw politicians abandon us. We stopped

doing public cornerstone layings. We saw young

men go elsewhere for friendships when they

found that our gatherings excluded some of

their friends. We stopped reaching out to our

communities for fear of having to answer embarrassing

questions.

The first part of our solution came a few years

ago when a young man moved to North Carolina.

The man was from Africa and came to our

state by way of Canada, where he had become a

Mason. He became the first black man (so far as

is known) to join one of our lodges.

When asked, "How many black members do

you have?" the dodge often used was, "We don't

know. " ere's nothing on our petitions that asks

about race."

It was another example of bending the truth

to our own purposes — a half truth that protected

us from our own bad behavior.

Today, in North Carolina, the old dodge is

the actual truth. We actually do not know how

many African American men we have in our

lodges. Not because we do not care, but because

it is becoming so common around the state.

" The other part of the solution is recognizing

the legitimacy of Prince Hall Freemasonry, allowing

them to move into the world of Freemasonry

where they belong, allowing us to stand alongside

one another. " at is finally done here, and by a

comfortable margin. In these 20,000 Prince Hall

Masons, we will find a hardy ally. "The cooperation

of our two grand lodges could well prove to be the

most powerful engine for positive influence in our

state. No two organizations have more good men

in more communities.

It was entirely appropriate, and perhaps as

Grand Master Cash has said, "by the hand of God,"

that Joseph Adegboyega's was the only hand Cash

saw when he asked for a volunteer to close Annual

Communication with the Closing Charge.

The multitude of Masons crowded forward to

the altar with Joseph to hear him speak some

of the most beautiful and instructive words of

Masonic teaching.

The voice of North Carolina's first black Mason,

the first black master of one of our lodges, rang

through the hall in all its rich African accent. It was

itself a symbol of the step North Carolina Masonry

has taken into the outer world, once again taking up

the mantle of pure Masonic teaching.

It is now for us, hand in hand with our Prince

Hall brothers, to move into our state's and nations'

future holding high the light of Freemasonry

for all to see and emulate: friendship, morality,

and brotherly love.

One of the great privileges of my life was being
permitted to call Most Worshipful Grand Master Milton F.
Fitch, Jr. and tell him the good news. My Grand Lodge had
finally recognized his Grand Lodge. The eleven year battle
was over.

Years before he had told me it wouldn't come about
overnight. It would be hard fought. It wouldn't come from
committees or edicts, it would only come about from one
Mason accepting another one at a time. He was right.

Soon after Recognition passed, my lodge had a joint
meeting with his lodge and as I looked around the room
filled with smiling faces both black and white all I could
think of was all those years we had allowed to pass us by. I

thought of the two great organizations and the good we could have done that will forever go undone.

THE END

Postscript

Was something learned from these eleven years? I don't know. A new battle is brewing on the horizon, a battle for others to fight in later years. Soon, 25% of the American population will be of Hispanic origin. Will they be our "new Blacks" or "new Irish"? Will some Masons one day see that these people are being excluded from Masonic lodges simply because of their heritage? To my knowledge, they have no Grand Lodge to recognize or even to ignore. To my knowledge, they have no group wanting to be seen as the good men they are. But, that is now, and that is to my knowledge. Who can tell about the things that are outside my scope of knowledge and the things to come? Because these eleven years began when just one man looked at things the way they were and said "This is wrong."

And too, Masonry continues to ignore over half the world's population. In Europe, female Masonry is taking root. Will it spread to the United States? I don't know, but I wouldn't imagine one would have to travel far to hear that "Female Masonry isn't real Masonry". Seem like I have heard that before.

Made in the USA
Columbia, SC
25 April 2021

36869695R00098